RGYALRONG:
conservation and change

Social change on the margins of Tibet

D A V I D   B U R N E T T

Lulu Publishing Services rev. date: 11/17/2014

DEDICATION

To the people of the Rgyalrong valley.

Contents

List of Illustrations

Preface

In 2006 I was invited to take up the position of Professor of Anthropology at the Institute of Education, Sichuan Normal University, Chengdu, Sichuan Province, People's Republic of China. My responsibilities were not only to teach Multi-cultural Studies to post-graduate students, but to help the Institute with their research projects in the west of the Province. The material in this book comes from many documents, student reports and research proposals that were produced during the seven years I lived and worked in Sichuan. I wrote this book so that the wealth of material might be made available to a wider readership.

A two hour drive from the provincial capital, Chengdu brings one to the beginning of the long climb up onto the Qinghai-Tibetan plateau, which eventually reaches Lhasa. The first day of driving takes one over the mountain ranges that run from north-south carved by the rivers that eventually feed into the River Yangtze. In this mountainous region on the margins of Tibet live several minority peoples such as the Qiang and Tibetans, together with the Yi and Bai in the more southerly province of Yunnan. Many students at Sichuan Normal University came from this region, and were training to become teachers in schools in this area.

The people of this region have faced many changes during the twentieth century, and have been left behind by the rapid economic growth that China has experienced since the late 1970s. The Institute of Education is interested in how schools, tourism and migrant labour to the cities were changing the culture of the local people. Nevertheless, there was a concern to help the people conserve their ancient culture. Questions were raised as to how the knowledge of traditional arts and skills might enable young people to find useful employment in a competitive job market. These studies therefore seek to address issues facing most societies in this global world, and fundamentally the question of how cultures may be conserved in a rapidly changing world.

I want to acknowledge my grateful thanks to the Institute of Education, Sichuan Normal University for their invitation to my wife and I to join the staff team for seven unforgettable years. Staff and students showed kindness and help in many practical ways as they willingly gave of their time. We will always remember the meals we enjoyed together, and the field trips into the mountain areas. Each trip seemed to turn into an adventure as we crossed mountain passes over 4,000 metres in altitude. There are too many people to name, but I must thank Professor Badeng Nima, Dean of the Institute of Education, who for many years has led the research projects among the Rgyalrong. His desire to help the young people of the minorities to develop their full potential in New China has stimulated all staff and students alike to achieve academic excellence and mutual respect. To all our dear friends Anne and I say, "Thanks for the memories".

David Burnett

1 Introduction

For many millennia people lived under much the same circumstances as their forebears, were little aware of historical change and scarcely differentiated past from present. Invaders may come and new kings rise to power, but the rural way of life of most people remained the same. Change was so slow that it would pass unnoticed in one lifetime. Then came what is known as the "Industrial Revolution", and change became obvious to the millions of people who migrated from the villages to the new factories in the growing cities. The past became clearly different from the present. There was a *then* and there is a *now*. How does one deal with the past? Lowenthal writes:

> The urge to preserve derives from several interrelated presumptions: that the past was unlike the present; that its relics are necessary to our identity and desirable in themselves; and that tangible remains are a finite and dwindling commodity. So swift is the pace of change, so conspicuously does the present differ from even the recent past, so precious and fragile seems much of our material legacy, that we forget how recent are the facets of awareness. (Lowenthal, 1993)

After the political and social upheavals of the twentieth century China is now doing much to preserve both the tangible and intangible culture of the nation. Many ancient sites such as the Great Wall, north of Beijing and the Terracotta Warriors of Xi'an have been renovated and have gained World Heritage status. Traditional art forms are being encouraged both as a valuable expression of intangible heritage and also as tourist attractions. This is encouraging many minority people to similarly explore their own distinctive traditions and art forms.

China is a land of many different ethnic groups of which the Han are the largest, consisting of some 91% of the entire population. It was in the 1950s that the new Communist government recognized 55 ethnic minorities or nationalities (*minzu*) that today number about 105 million people. These nationalities were defined in the way proposed by Stalin in 1913 for the minority people in the USSR. (Stalin, 1913). This was based on four criteria: the people are a historically stable community, they live in a defined geographical area, they have their own distinct language and also a distinct culture. In China a team of social scientists were assembled to list all the ethnic groups and from this wider list some 55 *minzu* were chosen. Questions still remain as to the definition of the various minorities. (Ma, 2010; Tang & He, 2010). Some communities who had earlier considered themselves distinct allied themselves with larger groups that had been recognized, and even today there are officially unrecognized groups that still remain. Today there are many university departments and research institutes on *minzuxue* ("ethnic studies") who annually produce a wealth of papers about these officially defined nationalities emphasizing their distinct attributes which mainly distinguish them from the majority Han. In the midst of observing "the other" it is all too easy to construct stereotypes of the people and their way of life.

Stereotypes of what it means to be Tibetan, for example, have been created in the popular media in China as well as in research publications. Tibetan dances are being adapted by Han Chinese to make them more accord to these stereotypes of what is considered *real* Tibetan, or what we will later discuss in this book as being *authentic*. In some of the universities in western China, Tibetan dancing has become popular to such an extent that Han students have taken over these activities much to the anger of the Tibetan students. In this way Tibetan culture is being reconstructed to the Han stereotype in what Stevan Harrell has called the Communist civilizing project (Harrell, 1998).

Harrell defines the civilizing project as the interaction of one people, the civilizing centre, with other groups (peripheral peoples) in terms of a particular kind of inequality. In this interaction, the inequality between the civilizing centre and the peripheral people has its ideological basis in the centre's claim to a superior cultural civilization. The effect of the civilization project on the peripheral people depends not just on the process, but the degree of complacency of the people in the project.

His framework of successive civilizing projects in China is helpful in understanding the enduring urge to civilize surrounding minorities as well as the nature of the content of each project. The first civilizing project he has called Confucian and relates to the late imperial Chinese state. This was based on *wenhua* (culture) being understood as a process of moral transformation through education, a process in which the civilizers were the *literati* elite perceiving the Han Chinese culture as the centre of world civilization. The second was that of Christianity which entered through western missionaries in the nineteenth century. As Harrell explains "the mission enterprise sought to bring not only the Gospel, but the modern life of Christian nations—with all its advantages in health, technology, and science—to the people of China". (Harrell, 1995:20). Finally there is the Communist civilizing project based on achieving modernity, understood as a stage in the universal unfolding of history through class struggle, and with the Party as the civilizer standing as a nation-state in competition with the world. One thing that the Christian and Communist processes had in common was the goal of transforming "ethnic minorities", especially those on the periphery.

The western world likewise has its own stereotypes of Tibet and Tibetans, which tend to revolve around the image of Shangri-la. (D. Lopez, 1998). Tibetans are recast as an exotic other, a spiritual people living in harmony with nature on the "roof of the world". Tibetan culture is often portrayed as an ancient spiritual civilization that is vanishing before our eyes. Unfortunately some Tibetans living outside

3

the country have used this stereotype for their own commercial gain or to attract a growing number of western disciples.

A different perspective for the Asian hinterland area has been proposed by James Scott in his book *The Art of Not Being Governed* (Scott, 2009). The argument he makes is that "the economic, political and cultural organization of (the peoples of *Zomia*) is, in large part, a strategic adaption to avoid incorporation in state structures" (Scott, 2009, 39). Braudel presents the idea of "an unbridgeable cultural gap between plains and mountains" (Braudel, 1993) and argues that hill peoples represent a reactive and purposeful statelessness of peoples who have adapted to a world of states by remaining outside their grasp. Scott uses the term "Zomia" for the peoples of the hills living in isolation from the civilizations of the fertile lowlands. The idea of Zomia comes from Van Schendel (2002) who argued for an increased interest on border areas with the distinctive cultures of the hill lands peoples. The region of Zomia can be considered as spreading from the hills of south-east Asia (Thailand & Burma) west across the Himalayas and northward into the eastern edge of the Tibetan plateau. As such, the Rgyalrong area would be seen as in retreat from the Han civilization of the plains. Scott's hypothesis is still being discussed as to how far it can actually be applied to such a wide and varied region of the world. However, it provides a useful model to discuss this form of cultural interaction.

The model rests on an implicit contrast between a powerful and oppressive state and the tribal peoples who resist and take refuge in the margins of the empire. However, as Michaud (Michaud, 2010) has argued, many people from the plains have moved to the highland towns that have now become centres of cultural hybridization. The indigenous population may sooner or later be integrated or overtaken by populations with outside origins making the distinct social space less relevant. The Chinese provinces of the Tibetan Autonomous Region (TAR) and Xinjiang offer thought provoking examples of this trend.

Many minority people are resisting the pressure of being assimilated into the modern world, and are seeking to retain their distinct identity by reinventing and embellishing many traditional cultural elements.

They now see themselves as being self-consciously distinct. They know politically they are nationals of new China, but they want to retain their own distinct identity. But, what is that identity and who defines it? From the different opinions found among Tibetans today, who can say what is the most valid interpretation, or whether there is any such thing as an authentic Tibetan culture?

This introduction considers two main aspects of the themes running through this book. The first is to provide an introduction to the people known as Rgyalrong (or *Gyalrong*, or in Chinese *Jiarong*) that are classed as part of the Tibetan *minzu* and the second is to explore the issues involved with cultural preservation. Preservation tends to be the word more commonly used in American English, whilst *conservation* seems more popular in British English. In this text these two terms will be used interchangeably, but more often the word conservation will be used as it better carries the notion of protection and caring. The over-riding question is how can the way of life of a minority society adapt to the impact of the modern world, as seen in the New China, whilst conserving its distinctive identity. One may question whether this even matters, as so-called primitive ways are disappearing under the impact of the modern. All societies are changing; let them change. However as Lowenthal realized the *present* needs the *past* to give meaning and hope for the future.

The Rgyalrong Valley

The so-called "Ethnic Corridor" runs along the eastern margins of the Qinghai-Tibetan plateau from the province of Gansu in the north, through Sichuan to Yunnan in the south. This is mountainous region with the Tibetan grasslands to the west and the plains of Sichuan to the east. For centuries this has been a place of cultural interaction among those identified as Tibetan and others as Chinese or Han. After the "Liberation of Tibet" by the People's Liberation Army (PLA) in 1950 the region was formed into four Chinese provinces: Gansu, Qinghai,

Sichuan and Yunnan. Within this geographical area are the river valleys of the Min and Dadu rivers among which the people called Rgyalrong live.

Rgyalrong is a shortened form of a Tibetan alliteration of '*Jia Mo Ca Wa Rong*'. '*Jia Mo*' refers to a queen, who according to legend ruled this area during the Tang dynasty (AD 608–917), and '*Ca Wa Rong*' refers to a river valley. The name therefore can be understood as 'The Queen's River Valley'. An alternative Tibetan transliteration is *gyalrong* and the people would be called *gyalrongwa* - the Chinese rendering is "Jiarong". Defining the term Rgyalrong has many difficulties. Rgyalrong is not a self-appellation but a loanword from Tibetan, the term by which outsiders refer to what could be regarded as "Rgyalrong-ness". The term can carry very different meanings, depending on whether it is defined by historical, political, or geographical arguments. I will use the term "Rgyalrong" to indicate both the historical and political entity of 18 Principalities and the area of distribution of the Rgyalrong language. This last usage of the term has only recently become more commonly used as a result of linguistic work published both inside and outside of China which uses the term in this rather narrower sense. Although the classification of Rgyalrong is still an issue of debate, it is becoming more widely accepted that Rgyalrong is a distinct language belonging to the Qiangic branch of the Tibeto-Burman family. There are currently an estimated 150,000–200,000 Rgyalrong speakers (Prins, 2006).

The valley was almost inaccessible until modern times being located at the southeast edge of the Qinghai-Tibetan plateau and separated from Sichuan province proper by the Alashan mountain range. The region consists of five deep valleys over 2000m above sea level and stretching for more than 200 km forming the pattern of a star with the county town of Danba at the centre. The main basin of the valley is formed by the river *Dajinchuan* (literally 'Big Gold River') that flows from the north in a southerly direction. At the point that it reaches Danba it merges with the *Geshizhaha* River and makes a sharp bend through gorges until it meets another large tributary, the *Xiaojinchuan* ('Little Gold River') which comes from the northeast. The river then becomes known as the Dadu River and runs southwards along a gorge so narrow that the river occupies the whole width of the river basin. There is a road on the west side of the river, but this is often washed away in the rainy season as the river floods or the rains cause rockslides

The people of Rgyalrong gained fame for their tenacity in fighting against the Manchu army in the eighteenth century, and later in their resistance to Communist control of the region (Karmay, 2005). In recent times they have been divided into two administrative areas: in the north is the Aba Prefecture and in the south, the Ganzi Prefecture. In total they may number as many as 100,000 persons. The present administration defines them all as part of the Tibetan nationality (*minzu*).

Chinese settlers now live in the main towns like Danba and Ma'erkang (alternatively written as Barkham) where modern style concrete buildings line the narrow valley basins. The majority of the Rgyalrongwa continue to live in distinctive houses in the rural areas often situated high in the mountains overlooking the main valley. The Rgyalrongwa do not have a writing system of their own, and their various dialects differ markedly from Standard (Lhasa) Tibetan. The main religious traditions of the region are generally classed as Bön ("black hat") and Gelugpa ("yellow hat") Buddhism. Temples and monasteries are found throughout the region as well as stupas constructed at significant points such as the joining of rivers or the crest of mountain passes. Another important religious feature of the Rgyalrong area is Mt. Murdo (or *dMu-rdo*, height 4820m), which is to the northeast of Danba town. Murdo is an important religious site for Bön as described by Karmay (Samten G Karmay, 1996). Every July people assemble at the Murdo Temple under the sacred mountain to celebrate the birthday of the god Murdo, and many people choose to circum-ambulate around the mountain in a quest to receiving blessing and good fortune from the deity.

Until recently the main economic activity of the region was timber, but the central government banned logging in the area in order to conserve the environment. The local authorities have therefore sought to introduce tourism as an alternative source of income. This has had two effects. First, young people have been attracted to the towns to entertain the tourists, and second, the people have become more aware of their own distinct way of life.

Conservation of culture

Staff and research students of the Institute of Education, Sichuan Normal University, Chengdu undertook a study of various aspects of the culture of the Rgyalrong valley and documented these in written and digital form. Their particular interest was to see how such traditional activities could be used to improve the quality of schooling of the local children, and to explore potential crafts that could bring employment into the area. The fact that they wanted an anthropologist on the team was for two reasons both mentioned by Sillitoe (Sillitoe, 2007). First, the Institute of Education recognized the knowledge that anthropologists have gathered through their fieldwork and the systematic engagement with contemporary theories. Second, the Institute wanted to apply the methods of anthropology especially the holistic approach, cultural relativism and participant observation. Nevertheless, this project continually gave rise in my own mind to the question of what is the particular contribution of anthropology to such an applied discipline. Is it merely a matter of helping to draw out "indigenous knowledge" or are there other factors involved? (Bicker, A. Pottier, J, Sillitoe, 2002).

In many cases, all that is left of "indigenous knowledge" are the memories of a few remaining members of the older generation who can recall the traditional stories, songs and dances. As Joy Hendry pointed out in *Reclaiming Culture* (Hendry, 2005) many communities that have been portrayed as "extinct", or almost so, are now reclaiming their cultural identity. The memories of the old people are becoming significant to the young in helping them understand who they are in the modern world.

Since the publication of Paul Connerton's book *How Societies Remember*, anthropologists have become increasingly interested in memory studies. (Connerton, 1989). Memory has often been viewed as having two distinct functions: to provide an accurate account of the past and to provide a so-called "usable past" that can be employed for some practical purpose in the present. It is easy to see these two functions as separate, but as Wertsch (Wertsch, 2002: 31) has pointed out they often operate in tandem, vying for position in any particular instance of remembering. Looked at in this way accurate representation should not be used as the only criterion to assess memory. Memory should also be assessed from the perspective of how effective it is in creating a usable past for contemporary generations in the midst of social change.

This approach has led to an exploration of "collective memory" as opposed to "individual memory". In this respect collective memory comes close to that of history, but as Halbwachs has shown on several accounts there is a distinction between the two. (Coser, 1992). He points out that collective memory tends to focus on the stability and continuity of a group and resists the idea that it has changed over time. In contrast, history is a record of changes in which that past is divided into discrete periods. Whilst collective memory tends to see things from a single committed perspective that reduces events to mythical archetypes, historians seek a critical discourse that is free from spontaneous memory. Wertsch has tried to tabulate the two, but he is conscious of the danger of such oversimplification (Wertsch, 2002:44).

Collective memory assumes that it reflects the unchanging essence of a group, and it is therefore less likely to recognize any transitions it may have undergone. However, given that collective memory emerges in response to a need to create a usable past, and this need varies over time, change will occur. What constitutes a usable past in one social context may be very different from that in another period.

Eliade in *The Myth of the Eternal Return* (Eliade, 1971) argues that members of "archaic societies" are characterized by a tendency to re-experience the past rather than remember it from a distance. They do this through repeated collective ritual performances that imitate an archetype. This does not mean, of course, that they are unaware of "history", but according to Eliade, they react against it. The recollection of historical events or individuals survives in popular memory for two or three centuries at the most. The historical figure can be assimilated into the mythical model of the hero, and the events identified with the category of mythical actions such as a fight with a monster. This is a theory that will be explored in chapters 9 and 10 with the restoration of two Rgyalrongwa festivals.

Finally, let us return to the question of why do people want to preserve the past? Lowenthal in *The Past is a Foreign Country* (Lowenthal, 1994) provides a useful starting point to this study before we explore the issues facing the Rgyalrong people. The past is integral to our sense of identity, and as we have already said this is a common driving force with many minority peoples in the face of global change. The past helps validate present attitudes and actions by affirming their resemblance to former ones. The past offers alternatives to an unacceptable present where a community might feel marginalized and excluded from the advantages of modern developments.

As Lowenthal reminds us, the past contains both dreams and nightmares. Nostalgia tends to be the word commonly used for a longing for the past perceived as a better age—even a golden age. History and memory so often glamorize the past such that the actual often leaves the modern generation disillusioned. Just as the revolutionary upheavals in France and the rule of Napoleon separated the old France from the new Republic, so the Communist revolution in China has separated the past from the present.

We cannot avoid remaking our heritage, for every act of recognition alters what survives. We can use the past fruitfully only when we realize that to inherit it is also to transform it. What our predecessors have left us deserves respect, but an attempt to simply preserve would become an intolerable burden. As Lowenthal writes: "The past is best used by being domesticated and by our acceptance and rejoicing that we do so. The past is not simply back there, in a separate and foreign country; it is assimilated in ourselves, and resurrected into an ever-changing present."

2 A Brief History

Long, long ago there was a country called *Zhang-zhung* (or *Shanshun*) that was ruled by a queen who lived in the stone castle which had a tower that was nine storeys high. The top of the tower was decorated with gold so that it shone in the sunlight. The influence of Zhang-zhung reached from northern Tibet to India in the south.

As the country prospered, the forest and the grassland began to suffer due to the increasing numbers of livestock. The queen received a message from an oracle telling her that in order to make the country prosperous again she must look to the east where there was a land that was fertile and had much gold. She decided that part of the royal clan should migrate to the east to look for this new land. When the clan migrated, they took with them soldiers, artisans and farmers along with their families. The royal clan moved east on the northern part of the Qinghai-Tibetan plateau until they reached the source of the Dadu River. They then travelled south along the river valley to where the land was fertile and gold could be found in the river. Here they stopped their journey. To the east of them steep mountains provided a natural barrier to the lowlands ruled by the Han people. Some stories tell of their fights with the local people, but eventually they settled in the valley where they built solid stone houses and set up a political system similar to that in their homeland. They called this place Rgyalrong—"the Queen's Valley".

Later, their home country of Zhang-zhung was conquered by the Tufan Tibetan Kingdom whose capital was at Lhasa, but the Queen's Valley in the east continued. With the advance of Tufan from the west and the Chinese dynasty from the east, the political system by which a queen ruled disappeared and men ruled.

This is one of the many legends concerning the origins of the people of Rgyalrong. This particular rendering of the story was chosen because it incorporates most of the common elements of the legend: an ancient homeland ruled by a queen, migration of the people, settlement along the gold river with the establishment of a similar way of life and buildings. Today, much of the early history is forgotten, and scholars are working to place the various elements together. Those written sources that do exist are in Chinese with some in Lhasa Tibetan, but there are none in the Rgyalrong language because it has only recently been reduced to writing.

The people known as Rgyalrongwa (or "Jiarong" in Chinese) live in the west of what is now Sichuan province in the mountain valleys along the eastern edge of the Qinghai-Tibetan plateau. The main valley of the region is long and narrow starting in the north with the confluence of *Duke He* (*rDo chu*) and *Make He* (*So mang chu*) rivers, to form the *Da Jinchuan* (Literally: Large Gold River). It flows southwards some 200 km to a place called *lCags zam* ("Iron bridge"), and from this point the inhabitants are Han and the river is known by the Chinese name of Dadu River. The iron suspension bridge is believed to have been constructed by a Tibetan engineer and marks the traditional border between Tibetans and Han Chinese. The linguist Van Driem in *Languages of the Himalayas* argued that the Tibetan word *rGyalrong* probably stands for "Sar rGyal-mo Tsa-ba Rong" or the "Eastern Queen's hot valleys" (Van Driem, 2001). The Chinese name Jiarong for Rgyalrong is a transcription of the Tibetan name. During the Qing dynasty the region itself was called Jinchuan (金川 Lit. "Gold River").

The French explorer Frederique Darragon argues that there is evidence to support the migration story (Darragon, 2006). The oral traditions all speak of Zhang-zhung in the region surrounding Mount Kailash in western Tibet as the origin of the people (Chogyal Namkai Norbu & D. Rossi, 2013). There are many words in the Rgyalrong languages like those of Zhang-zhung, and the phonological system in the Rgyalrong shares much in common with Ladakhi and Balti of western Tibet. The predominance of Bön traditions in the region also provides support for the migration story. According to the traditional Bön account of its origins, many thousands of years before the birth of the Buddha Shakyamuni, the Buddha Tonpa Shenrab Miwoche came to this world and expounded his teachings in the land of Olmo Lungring, which has been identified by some with Zhang-zhung (Karmay, 1986).

Qiang Belt

The Rgyalrong are part of what today is often referred to as the "Ethnic or Tribal Corridor" or "Qiang Belt" that runs along the eastern border of the Qinghai-Tibetan plateau. The first reference to the term "Qiang" is found in Chinese manuscripts dated during the Shang dynasty (1766–1045 BC) in which the term was used of a variety of peoples living to the north-east of the Chinese. Initially they appear to have been nomads since the Chinese character used for them is "Qiang" (Chinese 羌) consisting of the radical for a sheep above that for a man. According to this theory the Tibetan region was populated from this Gansu-Qinghai-Sichuan border region (Kapstein, 2006: 29). The history of the region is involved and complex, and was played out alongside the well documented events occurring to the east of the mountains in China. The first Chinese emperor Qin Shi Huang (Chinese 秦始皇, 259–210 BC) is supposed to have originated from the Qiang people in Gansu Province. Today the term "Qiang" refers to a distinct people (*minzu*) living in the Jinchuan region which was devastated by the magnitude 8 earthquake in May 2008.

The Han Dynasty (206 BC–AD 220) was founded by the peasant rebel leader Liu Bang (posthumously known as Emperor Gaozu). This period was one of Chinese cultural consolidation, economic prosperity and territorial expansion. Under Emperor Wu's reign (r. 141–87 BC), the Han Empire changed from having a relatively passive foreign policy to one that was offensive in order to deal with the increasing Xiongnu incursions on the northern frontier. In 133 BC, the conflict escalated into a full-scale war when the Xiongnu realized that the Han were about to ambush them at Mayi. The nature of the battles varied through time with many casualties and changes in control near the frontier regions. Regional alliances also tended to shift as one party gained the upper hand in a certain territory over the other. As the situation deteriorated for the Xiongnu, civil war erupted and weakened the confederation. Eventually, the Southern Xiongnu submitted to the Han Empire while the Northern Xiongnu continued to resist. Significant conquests over various smaller states finally resulted in the total victory of the Han Empire over the Xiongnu state in 89 AD. The Han Empire's political influence eventually expanded deep into Central Asia.

Although during the late Han (汉朝) dynasty (AD 25–220) Chinese influence had expanded to the edge of the Tibetan plateau, here it faced a radically different ecology. The Han could not cultivate the mountain terrain in the same way as the flat fertile plains of the Sichuan Basin. The ecological frontier therefore became a cultural and ethnic boundary. For this reason Wang Ming-ke argues, "When we trace the history of the Qiang, we are tracing not the native history of a non-Chinese people but a portion of the history of the Chinese (M.-K. Wang, 2002).

During the late Han (25–220) and Wei-Jin periods (221–419) a mixture of people were distributed along the mountainous fringe of the Qinghai-Tibetan plateau from the Kunlun Mountains in Xinjiang to southern Gansu, western Sichuan and northern Yunnan Provinces. The Chinese made some broad distinctions as to their identity: the Hu lived in the north, Di and Yi in the south and the term Qiang was used for others living in the region between.

An interesting construction dating from the third century AD is a "great wall" that is found near Wenchuan. This is an earthen wall built by the Han to make a clear divide between what they considered to be civilized society as opposed to the wild people (*lolo*) to the west. Van Driem argues that the *lolo* were one of five nomadic groups that overran China in the fourth century AD, but were later driven off and dispersed along the margins of the plateau (Van Driem, 2001). Some of these tribes were Tibetanized and other Sinized, and now make up part of the genetic make-up of the Tibetan or Han population.

There is some evidence that in the Rgyalrong area a Queendom did exist between the sixth-seventh centuries. In the latter half of the sixth century, the queen exchanged ambassadors with the central government of Han Chinese. Emperor Tang Taizong authorized the queen (Tangpang) with a Chinese seal and certificate of appointment. Empress Wu Zetian assigned the queen (*Lianbi*) as a general with her national defence department while brocade was presented to the queen to make clothes in local styles. The Queendom seems to have been a loose confederacy of many tribes, the biggest being merely 2,000 households. When Songtsen Gampo (Tubot) became powerful, some of the leaders secretly bowed to the house of Tibet and traded fabrics between the Han and Tibetan. The Chinese rulers were unhappy about this, but there was little they could do to put an end to it. Chinese records imply that the location of the Queendom was somewhere near the town of Danba in the centre of the region.

In 630, the Tibetan chieftain Songtsen Gampo (630–821) managed to unify the wild tribes of central Asia and form the Tibetan Empire (*Tufan*). Twenty years later he had raised one of the fiercest armies of all time and extended his empire eastward over Kham and Amdo, which had been the domain of the White Wolf Qiang, as well as most of central Asia. It was during this period that Zhang-zhung was probably conquered, but there is still confusion about the date and the events (Samten Gyaltsen Karmay, 1998).

The *Tufan* rapidly expanded eastward to the fringe of the plateau, and conquered the people along the ethnic corridor. This however, brought them into confrontation with the Han Chinese of the Tang dynasty (AD 618–907). It seems that Songtsen Gampo demanded tribute and a daughter in marriage from the frightened Chinese emperor. The emperor was obliged to comply. So powerful was the Tibetan Empire at this time that when in 763 a subsequent Chinese emperor refused to pay the fifty thousand rolls of silk owed in tribute to the Tibetan court, Trisong Detson (741–798 AD), Songtsen Gampo's great-grandson, invaded China and captured the capital of the Empire at Chang'an (modern Xi'an). The Tibetan king then deposed the Chinese emperor and replaced him temporarily with his own brother-in-law.

Later when King Tri Ralpachen (r. 815–838) converted to Buddhism the Tibetan empire began to disintegrate, and the eastern part of the plateau became more independent. In 821, during a lull in hostilities Tibet and China made a pact of non-aggression (Snellgrove, D. & Richardson, 1986). Although the political influence came to an end, Tibetan culture persisted along the ethnic corridor. This was because much of the area had come to be ruled by local chieftains who were, or were ascribed to be, descendants of the generals of the former Tibetan Kingdom.

As early as the Sui (581–618 AD) and the Tang (618–907 AD) dynasties, Chinese sources described a kingdom, ruled by a queen, where men had a secondary role. In the Chinese Annals, gold has frequently been linked with this kingdom where, similar to the legend above, it is said that "the queen lived in a nine storey (square) tower and the commoners in six storey ones". Paul Pelliot, the French Sinologist, suggested this semi-legendary kingdom may be associated with the Sumpi tribe, which might have been two kingdoms, one in the West, and one in the East (Pelliot, Paul & Chavannes, 1911). The Eastern kingdoms could have been located in the Rgyalrong area, where square towers are found in great number and where gold has been plentiful since historical times.

Another local legend links the "queen" with the native Bön goddess associated with Mount Murdo (*dMu-rDo*) near the modern town of Danba (Samten G Karmay, 1996). In the Tibetan sources, the Eastern Kingdom of Women is also often mentioned and the clan of the women rulers of this kingdom is called "*lDong*" (Stein, 1972). These people were classified by the Chinese as Qiang. Another variation on this legend of a Queendom had its eastern boundary at Ya'an, and was conquered by Songtsen-Gampo (605-649). The remnant exists as what is today known as the Zhaba who are found in the Ganzi Tibetan Autonomous Prefecture and number only about 8,000 persons (Hattaway, 1990). Although they have been Tibetanized they tend to be matriarchal not unlike the famed Mosuo of Yunnan.

Some scholars, such as Deng Tingliang, believe that the Rgyalrong are the direct descendants of a Qiang Tribe, the QingYi tribe. It is true that there are many cultural similarities between the Qiang and Rgyalrong, but there is little other evidence.

The Rgyalrong valley was a stronghold of the Bön religion, which is why some Japanese scholars believe that the Rgyalrongwa are the descendants of people from Zhang-zhung mentioned earlier. However, Karmay, a native of northern Rgyalrong and currently a researcher at the CNRS in Paris, disagrees with this interpretation (Samten Gyaltsen Karmay & Nagano, 2000).

The Ming dynasty (1368 to 1644) initiated sporadic armed incursions into Tibet during the 14th century, but the Tibetans successfully resisted these forays. The Ming did not garrison permanent troops in Tibet, unlike the later Mongol Yuan Dynasty. Emperor Wanli (r. 1572–1620) made attempts to re-establish Sino-Tibetan relations in the wake of a Mongol-Tibetan alliance initiated in 1578. Thus, by the late 16th century, the Mongols were armed protectors of the Dalai Lama with an increasing presence in the Amdo region, culminating in Güshi Khan's (1582–1655) conquest of Tibet in 1642.

The Eighteen Kingdoms of Rgyalrong

During most of the Ming (1368–1644) and the Manchu Qing (1644–1911) dynasties, the area, then called Jinchuan by the Chinese, was under the loose control of the Han Chinese. They recognized a *Tusi* (土司) system, which permitted local chiefs to rule as long as they paid tribute to the central government. Many Western scholars believe the establishment of the *Tusi* system marks the beginning of what Tibetan sources call the "18 kingdoms of Rgyalrong". Various lists of these kingdoms have been compiled usually based on Manchu reports, but the number and location seems to vary from one time to another. The number 18 probably comes from the fact that 18 is often a number of good fortune in Tibetan folk stories. The following picture taken in 2010 shows the restored palace of the *tusi* of Zhuokeji which is now a popular tourist attraction.

Restored palace of the *tusi* of Zhuokeji which was for a
period the headquarters of Chairman Mao in 1935.

Stein explains that the 18 Rgyalrong Kingdoms were recorded in Tibetan texts as populated by indigenous peoples whose names were *sBra*, *dBra* and sometimes *lDong*. The last name, as we have already seen, was also attached to the *Sumpi*, the queen of the Kingdom of Women and the Minyag. Following is a tentative list of the *Tusi* using the current Chinese name with Tibetan name in parenthesis:

1. Wassi: Near the Tuyu Shan Mountains centred about Tuyu Shan Hamlet of Yulong, near the modern town of Wenchuan.
2. Dzahgoo: Dzahgoo Valley (centred on Dzahgoonow, Lixian County).
3. Wori (Worhe) that is centred on Wori Township, Xiaojin County.
4. Xiaojin chuan *Tusi* centred on Meixing Town, Jinchuan County.
5. Chu Chen (Da Jinchuan *Tusi*) centred on Lhewu Hamlet, Jinchuan County.
6. Khro Skyals Chowsgya centred on Guanyinqiao (Goddess of Mercy's Bridge, Jinchuan County)
7. Gechizha (dGe bshes tsa) of Danba County, Ganze Prefecture
8. Badi (Pati, Blug Dee) of Danba County, Ganze Prefecture
9. Bawang (Bha Won) Danba County, Ganze Prefecture
10. Suomo (Swall Mo) around Dongsuomo Village, Ma'erkang County
11. Zhuokeji (Cog tse, Jogse Chogse) near Barkam (Ma'erkang County)
12. Dangba (Darnba) centred on Dangba Village, Barkam (Ma'erkang County)
13. Songgong (Soon Garn, Tsun Ghak) around Songgang Village, Barkam (Ma'erkang County)
14. Muping (Domb Ham Who) in Baoxing County, Ya'an
15. Ming Cheng (Ta Chien Loo, sMon rgyal) near Kangding, Ganze Prefecture)
16. Lengbian (Rab brtan) Lengji in Luding County
17. Shenbian around Shencun Village, Luding County

18. Khro chen Tien Chwan Lew Fan: Tianquan Township, Ya'an
19. Yuetoon (Maibeng) of Yutong district, Kangding County.

During the 19th century, Western explorers travelling in the Rgyalrong area reported the land was named "Mantze". This was how the Chinese called most of the lands of the Qiang Corridor at that time. Although Marco Polo never went to northwest Sichuan, he does mention a land of the Manzi and represents it on the map as all the southern lands under Mongol control. Marco Polo however never wrote about the distinctive towers and never ventured into the area even though his travels took him into nearby regions.

Frederique Darragon has argued that the existence of ancient towers indicates these kingdoms might date from before the Yuan Dynasty (1277–1367) (Darragon, 2009). She claims that most of the towers she has dated appear to be around 700 years old as will be discussed in chapter 5. These towers are usually located in villages within wealthy agricultural valleys that have the potential of being small kingdoms. Darragon also argues that since practically every district has their own distinctive dialect, this seems to indicate that each kingdom remained fiercely independent for a long period of time. None of these dialects have a written form and consequently there is no locally written history.

The region now called Rgyalrong was therefore sandwiched between the harsh Himalayas that became the cradle of the Tibetan Gelugpa culture and the rich lowland plains of the ancient Shu Kingdom in the Sichuan plateau. Between these two very different and expanding cultures, migrants, invaders and traders mixed and competed. The Rgyalrong population was probably a melting pot of different peoples and languages. It is what the Chinese call "*Tsa-kiu* 杂居 or tsa-tch'ou 独处" and the Tibetan old texts use to explain as a "land of horses, and people, all of motley colour" (Stein, 1972). This is well reflected in the eight or nine dialects currently spoken in this region, some of which are mutually unintelligible. Thus even today to communicate with people from the next valley most people use the Sichuan dialect of Mandarin especially now that Chinese is the medium of education in schools in the area.

The first exponent of the Gelugpa ("yellow hat") tradition known to have entered Rgyalrong was a disciple of Je Tsongkhapa (1357–1419) whose activities led to the formation of the Gelug School in the area around Lhasa. This disciple, known as Tsha kho Ngag dbang grangs pa, after completing his studies returned to his homeland in northern Rgyalrong. Little is known about him, but he is said to have come from the northern *tusi* of Xiaojin. He managed to convert a few people to the dGelug School and founded a few small monasteries, but it was not an easy task as the local people held strongly to the Bön tradition. During the following three centuries the inroads of dGelug was only small and growth often depended on the conversion of the local king. The change in attitude of the king often came about when a young boy of the king's family was "recognized" as a reincarnation of an important Gelug lama. Such a child therefore grew up to be the head of the Gelug monastery in the region, and so joined the local political and religious leadership in the family of the *tusi*. The kings of the northern *tusi* of Zhuokeji (*Cog tse*), Suomo (*So Mang*) and Songgong (*rDzong gag*) were eventually converted to Gelug, but only after many years. The Gelugpa, however had great difficulty penetrating into southern Rgyalrong where the kings were staunch up-holders of Bön. Thus, the Rgyalrong were divided between the ancient Bön and the newer Gelug tradition that was under the influence of Lhasa. This distinction is still noticeable even today as will be discussed in a subsequent chapter.

The Jiarong Wars

The Manchu people originated in Manchuria (today's north-eastern China). With the help of Ming rebels, they conquered the Ming Dynasty and founded the Qing Dynasty in 1644, which ruled China until the Xinhai Revolution of 1911. From 1720 the imperial court of the Manchu in Beijing was able to exert its political influence into Tibet. In appearance at least, the Manchu embraced the Gelugpa tradition of Tibetan Buddhism and presented itself as the defender of the new school. Throughout this period there were continued Mongol interventions in Tibet and a reciprocal spread of Tibetan Buddhism in Mongolia.

Emperor Qianlong (1711–99) was the fourth Emperor of the Manchu dynasty and reigned from 1736 to 1799. During his long reign he presided over a major expansion of the territory controlled by the Qing dynasty. This was made possible not only by Qing military strength, but also by the disunity and declining strength of many of the surrounding peoples. Under Qianlong, the Dzungars (or Zunghars) were defeated in 1755–58, and eastern Turkestan was incorporated into the empire and renamed Xinjiang.

An anti-Chinese revolt in Lhasa in 1752 was easily put down by Emperor Qianlong who sought to tighten his grip on Tibet by moving real power from the Dalai Lama to two Chinese high commissioners. This endeavour also brought to an end the incursions by Ghurkhas from Nepal on the Tibetan frontiers (1790–92). The Tibetans then agreed to pay regular tribute to Beijing and they came to consider the Manchu emperor as a manifestation of the Bodhisattva Manjusri.

In the south of what is modern China, military campaigns were less successful, but Chinese authorities continued to extend their domination. The first Qing encroachment into the Rgyalrong area began in 1746 on the pretence of settling local disputes in the *tusi* of Xiaojin. King Nam mkha' rgyal po of the neighbouring Dajin *tusi (chu chen)* encouraged resistance against the Manchu forces who finally abandoned the campaign in 1749.

The first Jinchuan campaign ended inconclusively. In a negotiated settlement in 1749, the Rgyalrong kings nominally submitted and pledged to send tribute to the Qing court, but they remained in control of their own regions. It was a bitterly fought battle with great casualties on both sides. The damage inflicted on the Rgyalrong was so great that it took several years for the region to recover. On the Qing side, three military commanders were executed for their incompetence in a campaign that had incurred great expense (Waley-Cohen, 1998:337).

After establishing their rule in Xinjiang the Chinese again turned their interests southwards. In 1771 a second military campaign was commenced against the Rgyalrong people. The Manchus once again made their main advance by the northern route from Wenchuan, but they soon became aware of the strong resistance.

At first, the Qing forces did not seem to be aware of the religious tensions among the Rgyalrong nor realize that many Rgyalrong were opposed to the dGelugpa tradition. The Bön leaders in Rgyalrong were however aware that the Manchus were supporters of the dGelugpa and its theocratic government in Lhasa and were eager to resist the advance. As the war dragged on, the Manchus began to wonder if the followers of Bön were performing some Bön rites against them. Emperor Qianlong was concerned that these rumours might have a negative influence on the morale of his forces in Rgyalrong. He therefore encouraged the dGelugpa lamas at court to perform rituals for the success of his army in the campaign. He also sought to gain the support of the Rgyalrongwa who followed the dGelugpa tradition.

The Bön Rgyalrongwa once again proved to be aggressive and stubborn. They were aided by their geographical location making the only access to the region through the long narrow river valleys. They also made effective use of their stone towers which was a form of warfare of which the Chinese had no experience. A key factor in the Manchu victory was the Portuguese Jesuit missionary named Felix da Rocha (1713–1781). He was employed by the emperor to manufacture cannons for the Manchu army. He even participated in the final assault against Dajinchuan (*Chu chen*) *tusi* that took place in 1775 when cannon balls were used to penetrate the defences of the castle. Finally, in 1776, Qing forces commanded by Agūi (1717-1797) triumphed (D. Martin, 1990). The Jinchuan leader, Sonom, was captured and executed, and his people came under Qing rule. Some 2000 people including the king of Dajinchuan (*Chu chen*) were taken prisoner to Beijing. Even today there is a community living not far from Beijing that is believed to be the remnant of these prisoners.

Dajinchuan *tusi* bore the major brunt of the conflict and was defeated. The Manchu army then went on to destroy Yungdrung Lhateng (*gYung drung lha steng*) the main Bön monastery of the *tusi* near the town of Anming. It was soon rebuilt on the same site, but this time in the style of a dGelugpa monastery and was invested with authority over all the dGelugpa establishments in the Rgyalrong region. Emperor Qianlong also issued an edict giving imperial support for the politico-religious domination by dGelugpa leaders in Rgyalrong and the purging of Bön.

These wars cost the Manchu government as much as 70 million taels, or 93 million ounces of silver. Emperor Qianlong calculated that the cost of the Jinchuan Wars was more than twice the amount spent to conquer Xinjiang,a vast area perhaps twenty times larger than the Jinchuan region. "Pacifying Yili, securing the Hui region, those were great endeavours!" the emperor declared. "Yet the cost did not reach thirty million taels, nor did it take five years. But those two wars with those little Jinchuan bandits, whose land does not cover 500 li, and who number fewer than 30,000, cost us seventy million taels and took five years!" (X. Wang, 2011).

The kingdom of Zagu (near Luxian) was the largest and most powerful of the *tusi*, so Qianlong decided to execute the king and divided it into four smaller kingdoms. In this way he permanently weakened the kingdoms. Wassi then became the most powerful of the Rgyalrong kingdoms, but overall the Rgyalrong *tusi* never again became a major political force.

New Bön Tradition

Although the eighteenth century was a period of warfare and political unrest there was a revival of Bön tradition in Rgyalrong. One of the most influential figures in this movement was Kun grol grags pa

(1700–c1766). After a difficult childhood Kun grol eventually set out in 1724 on pilgrimage to Central Tibet. When he arrived in Lhasa the people were in great fear because of the anticipated arrival of the Mongol army, and so he travelled on to the major monasteries in the west of the country. Here his mentor was Sangs rgyas gling pa (1705–1735), a mystic from the Kham area who is known for opening up Mount Murdo as a sacred place and centre for pilgrimage. He encouraged Kun grol to revive the Bön tradition in Rgyalrong, which he sought to do even during the periods of warfare.

Today, Bön is often classified into three traditions: Old Bön, Yungdrung Bön and New Bön. The oldest tradition of Bön is Shamanistic based on the concept of a world pervaded by good and evil spirits; it is believed to have originated in the land of Olmo Lungring and was introduced into the ancient Kingdom of Zhang-zhung. Following Songtsen Gampo's conquest of Zhang-zhung and unification of Tibetan tribes, he introduced Buddhism as the chosen religion and the popularity of Bön declined. The second tradition of Yungdrung, also known as "Eternal Bön" is dedicated to perpetuating the teachings of their founder Tonpa Shenrab Miwoche, who occupies a pre-eminent position in Bön religion similar to that of Shakyamuni in Buddhism. New Bön began in the 14th century when some Bön teachers discovered *termas* (texts) related to Padmasambhava. Although the practices of New Bön vary to some extent from Yungdrung Bön, the practitioners of New Bön still honour the Abbot of Menri Monastery as the leader of their tradition.

The new Bön tradition was ideally suited to the situation in Rgyalrong which was experiencing the pressure to convert to the Gelugpa tradition. Kun grol was recognized by his master as a text rediscoverer (*terma*). Sangs rgyas gling pa and Kun grol arrived in Rgyalrong in 1733, and had protection from the monk-prince of the dGe bshes tsa kingdom, and through this connection contacts were made with the kingdoms of Khro skyabs and Chen. Kun grol made a number of visits to Rgyalrong, but these had to stop during the period from 1746 to 1749 owing to the first Manchu incursion. After the conflict he resumed making visits to the region. In 1751 he completed a detailed catalogue of the Bön Kanjur in the palace of the Rab brtan. He also wrote many texts, and is generally thought to have died about 1766, but this date is uncertain.

Rgyalrong under Qing Dynasty

In 1797, Emperor Qianlong issued an edict in support of the new dGelugpa monastery of gYung drung lha steng, and encouraged the spread of dGelugpa tradition among the Rgyalrong. From this time most of the abbots of this monastery were appointed from dGelugpa monasteries in Central Tibet. It was an abbot of the gYung drung lha steng who later in 1874 converted the old Bön monastery called Bar Khams gYung drung gling into a dGelugpa monastery and gave it the name dGa'Ildan dar rgyas gling. This time the old temple was not dismantled, but the Bön paintings were painted over and dGelugpa figures painted on the walls.

Following the triumph of the Qing forces in 1776, the Qing enforced their control even though they allowed the continuation of the *tusi* system. Many of the Rgyalrong kingdoms had lost much of their population through the war or they had been taken captive. This left some of the regions in the Dadu River valley almost unpopulated, and so in the early nineteenth century some of the Qiang people were encouraged by the Chinese to move into these regions and act as overlords. This resulted in a marked social divide between the Qiang settlers and the remaining Rgyalrong. The antagonism between these groups can still be sensed even though they have similar cultures and generally live in harmony. The result is that today communities of Qiang exist in the main valleys of the Dadu River, and there is no clear boundary.

About this time a new social identity emerged in the region that came to be known as Khampa, and it was with this identity that the history of the Rgyalrong area was hereafter to be associated. The

Khampas began to be regarded as a distinct group by both the Tibetan and Chinese following the campaigns of Nag-sked Mgon-po rnam-rgyals (often known as Amgon) (Coleman, 2002). Amgon was the chief of a tiny tribe of about 60 families from Nyarong (Xinlong) county who over a period of 30 years gained supremacy over all the kingdoms from Chamdo to Kangding. This expansion was possible because at this time China was preoccupied with the two Opium Wars with the British (1839–1842 and 1856–1860) and the Taiping Rebellion (1851). Tibet was also involved in conflicts with the Dogras (1841) and the Gurkhas (1850-1856) who dwelt to the south of Lhasa.

In this power vacuum Amgon succeeded in creating a new alternative political entity of Kham. The governor of Sichuan was unable to prevent this and in February 1863 the Tibetan government was forced to intervene with a strong military force and through deceit and treachery managed to kill Amgon. However, the Tibetan victory opened Central Tibet to another incursion of the Manchu dynasty. While he was alive Amgon was both hated and feared, but after his death he became something of a folk legend. More significantly this resulted in the people of Kham region losing trust in the Central Tibetans.

It was during this short period that the Kham influence spread through the southern part the Rgyalrong valley. Kangding is not too distant from the *tusi* of Danba, Bawang and Badi north along the Dadu River. South are the *tusi* around Luding, and the ancient border with the Han. The ruling elite of this region intermarried with the Kham leading families, and came to see themselves as Kham rather than Rgyalrong.

British attempts from India to open relations with Tibet precipitated the British invasion of 1903–1904 led by Francis Younghusband (French, 1994). In 1904 there seemed a real possibility that Tibet could become a British protectorate as had Bhutan and Sikkim, so for the first time China made a concerted effort to bring Kham under their control.

In 1905, the Chinese made a decree in Batang that reduced the number of Tibetan monks in the monasteries and granted land to French Catholic priests. This resulted in an uprising led by the monks, which led to swift retaliation by the Chinese army. They retook Batang and destroyed the monastery. They appointed Zhou Erh-Feng to continue the work of "consolidation", which he did with such ruthlessness that he earned for himself the nickname of "the butcher of monks". Two thousand of his troops then marched on Lhasa, but when his advanced guard arrived they found that the Dalai Lama had already fled to India.

Having subjugated Eastern Kham by 1908, Zhou unveiled a plan to consolidate the whole of Kham under direct Chinese administration. All of Kham as far west as Giamda (150km east of Lhasa) was to be a separate province to be called Xikang (西康省 Xīkāng Shěng) with its provincial capital at Kangding. China wanted to secure a buffer territory as large as possible in case Tibet became a foreign protectorate. China hoped that this new boundary would become accepted as the frontier between China and Tibet. However, before the plan could be fully implemented, the Qing dynasty fell in a revolution that plunged China into chaos for the next 15 years. By mid-1912 the Chinese had lost control of most of the frontier districts.

Kham under the Nationalist Government

Britain was becoming concerned about Chinese expansionism and threats to British interests, so in late 1913 they pressured China to join Britain and Tibet in tripartite talks in Simla (India) to settle the question of the Sino-Tibetan frontier and Tibet's political status. As a result all Chinese were expelled from Kham (1913–1919), the frontier was moved to the Dadu River, east of Kangding, and Lhasa officials were allowed to administer Kham. (Convention Between Great Britain, China, and Tibet, Simla 1914).

From 1916 until 1928 China was politically divided under several military warlords. In 1918, a Sichuan Chinese warlord named Peng advanced across Kham, in the direction of Lhasa. The Tibetan troops were much better trained than those who had faced Zhou Erh-Feng and to Peng's surprise and humiliation they drove him back, and after months of fighting he was forced to surrender and repatriate

3,000 Chinese prisoners via India. Tibetan troops subsequently moved eastward towards Kangding where they threatened to take more prisoners and even invade the Sichuan Basin. Hastily the Chinese called on the British to use their influence to prevent a further advance of the Khampas into China. The British did this by cutting the supply of arms and ammunition filtering into Tibet by way of Kalimpong, and soon the Kham had used all their ammunition. They then sent Eric Teichman, a British Consular officer to Kangding to negotiate with the Khampas. On August 19th 1918 a peace treaty was signed that provided for the acceptance of a provisional boundary roughly along the Yangtze, and a demilitarized zone established between the Yangtze and the Dadu rivers (Madsen, 2010).

In 1928, the Nationalist government revived the plan to form two new provinces, the Xikang, with Kangding as its capital, covering most of Kham and Qinghai, encompassing all the region of Amdo. Because neither the Khampa nor Lhasa authorities published maps or were represented abroad, these claims were never refuted. Most Chinese history books cover the creation of Xikang, but do not mention the negative response of the Khampas.

In 1928 the chief of Beri rose in arms against the Lama of Nyarong, and Targye monastery, resulting once again in war. General Liu Wen Hui, a new Sichuan warlord, took the opportunity of sending troops into the demilitarized zone to support the chief of Beri. As soon as Liu's troops were involved, the Khampa troops from Derge attacked the Chinese soldiers. It took five months of bitter fighting before the Khampas were able to drive the Chinese troops out of most of the Kham region. Their success was short lived as Liu Wen Hui was able to regroup and counterattack by the end of 1931. By May 1932 the Tibetan forces had been driven out of Ganzi and Nyarong, and by July they had lost Derge, which the Tibetans had held since 1919. Soon afterwards they were forced to pull back to the Yangtze River itself.

Liu Wen Hui was making ready to advance further west when he was threatened from the rear. His nephew Liu Xiang who was also a warlord marched on Kangding in a bid for supremacy. Liu Wen Hui had no alternative but to withdraw his troops and return to Kangding. In the aftermath of these events an agreement was reached. On 10th October 1932, Liu and the Tibetan leaders signed a truce in which it was agreed that the Tibetan forces would remain west of the Yangtze River and the Chinese would remain east of it. The river remained the *de facto* border between Tibet and China until October 1950.

During the famous "long march" various divisions of the Red Army passed through the Dadu valley in 1936. At the iron bridge in Luding, Chinese historians claim that a crucial battle took place. According to the story, by the time the Communists got to the bridge in May 1935 it had all of its planks removed and was guarded by a regiment of Kuomintang soldiers armed with machine guns. At night 22 brave Communist commandos, climbed across the bridge, in some places hanging from the chains and pulling themselves forward hand over hand with grenades in their teeth. They captured the bridge to allow the marchers to proceed. Mao later told Edgar Snow that the crossing of the Dadu River was the single most important event of the Long March. (Snow, 1978). It was said that of the 80,000 soldiers that began the march in 1934, 20,000 made it across Luding Bridge. More recently Chang and Halliday have claimed that the story was in fact a fabrication invented by Mao to impress the journalist (Chang, Jung. Halliday, 2005:158).

The Red Army continued up the Dadu River valley amidst opposition from the local people. At Xiaojin two divisions of the Red army met and Mao used the small Catholic Church as his headquarters for 14 months. This church is now a heritage museum for the Long March. The two armies, totalling 90,000 men were crowded into the Tibetan valley that was barely able to sustain its own population. The soldiers were reduced to fighting for food with the local people. The Tibetans hated the Reds and launched guerrilla attacks from the forest killing many of the stragglers (Chang, Jung. Halliday, 2005:165).

In 1937 the Red army moved northwards and faced fierce opposition from the *tusi* of Zhuokeji which was at that time in alliance with Kuomintang. Later the king changed allegiance to support the

Communists and was granted various benefits. However, in 1967 during the Cultural Revolution this was forgotten and the king was killed as being an enemy of the people. Sun Mingjing has compiled a fascinating photographic record of Xikang during the period 1939 to 1944 (Sun Mingjing, 2009).

New China

On October 1st 1950, the Chinese Communist Party came to power and established the People's Republic of China (PRC). A week later on the 7th October 1950, 40,000 PLA troops advanced into Tibet in a surprise night attack to trap the Tibetan army in a pincer movement that would prevent any retreat to Lhasa. In the north the 54th regiment crossed the Yangtze above Dengke, by-passed the Tibetan army at Kbyungpo and were able to attack Riwoche. From there they marched south, and encircled the Tibetan army, cutting off their escape route. In the south the Chinese 157th regiment attacked on 7th/8th October. After crossing the Yangtze River in force and overpowering the Tibetan outposts there, they pushed towards Ma'erkang where Derge Sey surrendered his entire force of over 400 troops. There was no possibility that the Tibetan army could stop the PLA advancing towards Chamdo and so the new Governor of Kham decided to evacuate. Eventually the Chinese took Riwoche and encircled the retreating Tibetan troops near Drukha Monastery, and the Tibetans surrendered to the PLA on 19th October 1949.

The Chinese could have marched straight on to Lhasa, but the repercussions would have been far-reaching. Instead they convinced the Tibetan government to sign a seventeen-point agreement. Although Mao Zedong's ultimate aim was to transform Tibet in accordance with socialist principles, between 1951 and 1959 no aristocratic or monastic property was confiscated, and feudal lords were permitted to exercise judicial authority over their hereditarily bound peasants.

The situation was very different in the Kham and Amdo regions as these Tibetans were not part of what Mao regarded as "political Tibet" (Tibetan Autonomous Region, TAR) nor part of the Seventeen-point Agreement. "Democratic reforms" started as early as 1952–53. More roads were built, with the aid of large numbers of Chinese workers. In order to feed them, the Chinese started to "borrow" and then buy stocks of food, causing severe inflation. Large numbers of Chinese settlers were brought into the Chamdo area, and PLA soldiers were encouraged to marry local Tibetan girls and settle down and have families. In places, those who resisted the Chinese were rounded up, labelled as "reactionaries and serf-owners" and were publically executed.

From 1952 the Chinese began sending Tibetan children, sometimes forcibly, from Eastern Kham, to study in Beijing or Chengdu. More than 30,000 children were sent to Han China between 1952 and 1969. The rigorous programme of education in Communist teaching and the Chinese version of Tibetan history provoked the Tibetan students in Beijing into an intense awareness of their own national identity. Between 1956 and 1957 they openly revolted, but were subdued with an "anti-local nationalism" campaign. This coincided with the "hundred flowers" era in China.

In late 1955 the Chinese authorities levied large taxes on traders returning from India and ordered the monks of Litang Monastery to produce an inventory for tax assessment. The monks refused to oblige and called on the village headmen to take up arms against the communists. In February 1956, the Chinese laid siege to the monastery which was defended by several thousand monks and farmers, and after the Chinese had lost two divisions they took a decisive step to bring the siege to an end. Ilyushin 28 type warplanes were flown from the Sichuan plain, and with terrible and swift vengeance Litang monastery and the surrounding area was bombed and machine-gunned reducing it to rubble. Two thousand fighters and monks escaped, and another two thousand surrendered. The Chinese bulldozed the whole town flat (Lane, 1994). This was one of a series of uprisings against Chinese rule, which spread to Batang, Derge, Chamdo and Ganzi. The Khampas united and prepared to retaliate even though they were continually menaced from the air.

This was augmented on the ground by a large Chinese offensive, as one by one the Chinese began to retake towns and villages. Every day the ranks of the Khampa guerrillas grew and harassment of Chinese positions was renewed. Stories are told that in some towns, re-conquered by the Chinese, the communists tortured monks, abbots were lashed to horses and dragged through the street, and children were forced to shoot their parents. Between 1956 and 1957 over 4,500 people were killed in the Ganzi area alone (Peissel, 1972).

Nothing seemed to weaken Khampa resistance, and Chinese were not safe anywhere in the region. In July 1956 Vice-Premier Marshal Chen Yi was sent in person to investigate. Not only did the Marshal see the situation for himself but his party was attacked and ambushed by Khampas. Chen Yi escaped with his life, but he lost 300 of his men. This sobering welcome caused the Chinese government to swallow its pride and make peace overtures and they began to negotiate directly with the rebels. For the Khampas it was a great moment, and towards the end of September the fighting abated. The Khampa commander began drafting a 10-point agreement including the postponement of reforms for at least six years, the withdrawal of Chinese troops from Tibet and respect for Tibetan autonomy covering the entire ancient realm of Songtsen Gampo. The Chinese agreed to these terms, which were publically confirmed in the Chinese Press.

The Khampas rejoiced, unaware that the whole operation was a trap. The Chinese gained a much needed lull in the fighting and a way of persuading the Dalai Lama to return to Lhasa. When the Dalai Lama reached Lhasa the Chinese reconfirmed that "reforms" would be postponed and the Chinese troops withdrawn, publically repeating the articles of the Khampas' agreement, but this time with some modifications. The Chinese asserted that the Khampa agreement concerned only Tibet west of Chamdo - in other words TAR. The Chinese moved the troops who had been stationed in Central Tibet into Kham to fight and soon Eastern Kham was annexed to Sichuan Province.

Infuriated, the Khampas rose up again with renewed violence, but the Lhasa government was no longer willing to support Eastern Tibet as they were more concerned with maintaining their fortunes and privilege under Chinese rule. The Khampas were convinced that to succeed they must by all means overthrow the ruling clique in Lhasa and take over the leadership of Tibet. Thus, while maintaining their positions in Kham they began to infiltrate central Tibet, determined to persuade the peasants to rise and join them in the ultimate battle for their common race.

It is not known how many lost their lives in Kham during these years; many more were to die in the famines of 1960–61. By 1961, refugees reported a staggering drop in the male population, as if two whole generations had been annihilated. In the region of Golok the population in 1957 was 120,000, but between 1958 and 1962, 21,000 local Tibetans were killed fighting the PLA. 20,000 more were executed in local prisons, and a further 20,000 died as a result of famine. Of the original population only 6,000 remained between 1963 and 1979. In 1979, new Settlers, mostly Chinese were brought in to increase the population to 10,000.

In Lhasa the traditional hardliners felt that they had been forced into the agreement with China through the invasion of Chamdo and were not really bound by its terms. They used the food shortages, mainly created by the influx of large numbers of Chinese troops, as a means to persuade the Chinese to withdraw all but a few troops and officials. This was the same strategy they had used in the eighteenth century with the Qing dynasty garrisons. By the mid-1950's the situation inside Tibet began to deteriorate as Chinese Communists tried to institute "reform" and Tibetan hardliners and Khampa fighters began organizing an armed rebellion.

Most of the Khampas, who infiltrated or drifted into Lhasa, subsequently moved south to Lhoka. It was in the south that the famous *Four Rivers and Six Ranges* resistance group emerged. Its name came from the ancient name of Kham, and was formed under the leadership of Gonpo Tashi Andru-Tsang. Fighters from all over Tibet joined the Khampa movement. The Khampas saw force as the only solution, the Dalai Lama and the monastic community condemned it while the Tibetan government hoped to achieve an appeasement. In 1957, the USA was beginning to train and arm Khampa guerrillas. Mao made a last attempt to salvage his gradualist policy when in 1957 he reduced the number of Han cadres and troops in Tibet and postponed socialist land reforms for 6 years, or until conditions were suitable.

The Chinese failure to put down the rebellion in Kham and the subsequent victorious advance of the guerrillas into Lhoka obliged the communists to revise their attitude towards the Khampa uprising. The Chinese tried to further exploit the mistrust between Central Tibetans and the Khampas. The Chinese sought by any means to revive the spectre of the Khampas as bandits and rivals of Lhasean sovereignty. Chinese secret police were sent to hunt down the rebel leaders, and Khampa refugees were attacked by Chinese soldiers or shot at by spotter planes. Such repressive measures had the opposite effect from that hoped for by the Chinese, as increasing numbers of Central Tibetans joined the Khampas in Lhoka.

In Eastern Kham and Amdo, Chinese repression was reaching a climax as fifteen thousand babies and young children were forcibly deported "in order that their parents could do more work". Any parents who protested were thrown into the river or threatened with execution. This caused even more refugees to make their way firstly to Lhasa, and as a result of secret police harassment, on to Lhoka. All over Tibet the guerrilla forces were active.

In the last months of 1958 Khampa leaders repeatedly approached the Tibetan cabinet urging them to stand up in defence of their common cause. Each time the delegations were instructed to return to Kham and make peace with the Chinese. The Khampas patience wore out and in December they attacked two Chinese garrisons less than 30 miles from Lhasa and made one last appeal to the Dalai Lama. His failure to back the Kham fighters and lack of comprehension of the situation resulted in the Khampas deciding that the time had come for them to act.

At the beginning of Feb 1959 Radio Beijing announced that the Dalai Lama was to attend the National People's Congress in Beijing. Given that the Dalai Lama had not formally accepted the invitation this alarmed most Khampas. They were concerned that as in 1954, he would be kidnapped and used as a propaganda tool. In this highly charged atmosphere the Dalai Lama received a direct invitation—by-passing normal protocol—to attend a theatrical performance alone in the Chinese headquarters. Rumours soon spread that the performance was a trap. Crowds of people set out for the *Norbulinka* (Summer Palace) to prevent him going to the Chinese camp. Among them were hundreds of fully armed Khampas. The abduction scare provided the Khampas with the opportunity for forcing the Dalai Lama and his ministers into opposition to the Chinese, and consequently they took over leadership of the crowd. They formed a Freedom committee and immediately made clear their intention of taking over the cabinet and forming a new government. They ordered a unit of heavily armed Khampas to surround the *Norbulinka* and replace the Dalai Lama's bodyguard. The Dalai Lama and his entourage suddenly realized that they were no longer leaders of Tibet and they would have to negotiate directly with the Freedom Committee.

At nightfall on 17th March 1959 dressed as a Khampa soldier the Dalai Lama and a small group were smuggled out of the palace, initially to Lhoka and eventually into exile in India. The Chinese did not suspect anything until the following day. In their efforts to locate the Dalai Lama the Chinese let it be known that they would, if necessary, bombard the summer palace. This angered the crowds, who were still unaware that the Dalai Lama had left the palace. The people were indignant and this reignited their old hatred of the Chinese (Goldstein, 1997). Monasteries were then dissolved and monks were put to work. By 1959 only 36 aged-monks remained out of the 500 previously resident in Sakya monastery. Monasteries, castles and historic buildings were systematically destroyed and national festivals and celebrations were banned. It is estimated that between 1955 and 1959, 65,000 Tibetans were killed and in the year following the uprising, 87,000 Tibetans were executed in Central Tibet alone. Writers continue to discuss the motivation and value of the rebellion that has so marked the history of Tibet (Dawa Norbu, 1979).

The Rgyalrong region was to be overwhelmed by another vast movement during the Cultural Revolution of 1966–76. Red Guards marched up the valley of the Dadu River to Danba. On their way they destroyed many of the towers especially those near the towns and river. The Red Guard also damaged many temples including the bsTan phel gling dGelugpa monastery that had previously enjoyed the support of the Manchus. At the beginning of the 1980s, the local Bönpa people reclaimed the monastery and the Sichuan government finally permitted them to rebuild it as a Bönpa monastery.

During the height of the Cultural Revolution, official persecution extended to religious practices even those observed in the homes of ordinary Tibetans. People were forced to denounce the Dalai Lama, and pictures of him were burned in the streets. Private altars, prayer wheels, prayer beads and amulets were destroyed. According to the former cadre Dhondub Choedon:

> The Red Guards had the goal of destroying the Four Olds and establishing the Four News. The Four Olds: old thought, old culture, old habits and old customs. The Four News: new thought, new culture, new habits and new customs. The Four Olds are the things Tibetan and the Four News are whatever the Chinese say...the Chinese and the Red Guards charged that all Tibetans keeping old objects were guilty of trying to resurrect the past, that they were the enemy within (Quoted in Kolas & Thowsen, p.48).

* * * * *

The CCP has firmly stressed the unity of the Chinese nation while acknowledging what eventually became 55 minority nations (*minzu*). Along the Qiang belt, the distinction of nationalities basically followed the ancient Qing concepts of Qiang, Fang and Yi. Most of the people called Fang are now classified as the eastern-most section of the Tibetans (*Zang zu*). The people in the southern end of the belt were designated as being the northern-most part of the *Yi zu*. A Qiang nationality was formed in the middle even though the population was relatively small, comprising of only about 200,000 people. The inhabitants of the Rgyalrong valleys have, as most of the populations who practice Buddhism or Bön, been attached the Tibetan Minority (*Zang zu*), with whom they share many customs and many words. The Rgyalrong region is now divided politically: The northern area is the Aba Autonomous Prefecture with its centre at Ma'erkang (Barkham) and the southern part, which begins just south of Chuchenrdzong, is Ganzi Autonomous Prefecture with its centre of administration in Kangding.

3 Land

The western escarpment of the Sichuan Basin is formed by the Daxue Shan range, which marks the transition zone between the Chinese plains and the Tibetan highlands. The range is an important boundary, not only climatologically and ecologically but also in ethnic terms (Thomas, 1999). The valleys of the mountain ranges require a totally different form of agriculture to that of the plains. As a result there is a very different way of life between the Han farmers and the Rgyalrong, Yi and Qiang.

As mentioned in chapter 1 the Rgyalrong people reside along two major rivers, the Dadu and the Min both of which flow in a southerly direction. The Min River starts in north-central Sichuan, where its basin is limited by the Qionglai Mountains in the west and the Min Mountains in the east. The river passes through the Longmen Range and enters the plains of the Sichuan Basin near the city of Dujiangyan where the famous ancient irrigation system is located. The Dadu River originates from the Guoluo Mountains on the border of Sichuan and Qinghai provinces with the confluence of the *rDo chu* (Dokong) and *So mang chu* (Markog). The river then flows through the valley of Tsha Kho and 200 km downstream is known as the Dadu (大渡河) in Chinese. Here the valley widens at a place called "Iron Bridge" after which point the inhabitants are mainly Chinese. The iron suspension bridge is said to have been originally constructed by Tibetan engineers, and this has traditionally marked the Chinese-Tibetan border in the area. The Dadu River converges with the Min River at Leshan, where the famous Giant Buddha statue commands a grand view of the rivers.

The Kham region is one of the most unique biological regions on Earth. As Studley writes:

> Kham's spectacular north-south mountain ridges, sandwiched between deep river gorges, contain the most diverse vascular plant flora of any region of comparable size in the temperate zone, and almost half of China's flowering plant species (Studley, 2007: 27).

A Sacred Land

The Rgyalrong region has long been considered as one of Tibet's "hidden lands" (*sbas yul*). The term refers in Tibetan sacred geography to an inaccessible place. From the thirteenth century onwards there were sporadic attacks by Mongol forces throughout the country, attacking anything in their way. Due to this threat, a body of literature came into existence warning of the "Hor", a term of reference for the Mongols. Rgyalrong was one of the few places where the people resisted the Mongols, and later they similarly opposed the Manchu. In winter, snow made the passes inaccessible and in summer the heavy rains often caused the rivers to overflow their banks and wash away the road that ran alongside the west bank of the river. This made the region isolated from the outside world for much of the time.

It was also considered a hidden land because it was the place where spiritual masters claimed to have discovered "hidden texts" (*terma*), especially in the area around Mount Murdo. For the Bönpa, these texts are believed to have been concealed by famous teachers in earlier times and have been discovered by text revealers, or *terton,* who visited the region to find these hidden texts. The Bönpa sage Dran pa nam mkha and his Buddhist disciple Variocana are also believed to have dwelt in a cave in the vicinity of Mount Murdo in the eighth century, but no records have been found that go back beyond the 14th century.

As most of the mountains are seen as the residence of the deity of the local territory (*yullha*), mountain sites were often chosen as suitable for concealing religious texts. The local deity is then recognized as "the guardian of the treasure" and the place is considered sacred. When a treasure is excavated the place may become even more sacred, but to obtain this highest status it must be instituted by a man of spiritual power who will trace out a foot-path for circumambulation around the mountain, and identify various places along the path. He will designate the last day of the tracing out of the route as the day for the annual celebration, and will write a guide for the holy mountain. The mountain therefore becomes a place of circumambulation for all those who seek blessing. Mount Murdo is the most significant peak of the Rgyalrong region rising to 4820 meters. The mountain was "opened" by Sangs-rgyas gling-pa, and the annual celebration takes place on the 10th day of the 7th month of the Tibetan calendar (Samten G Karmay, 1996).

Matthew Kapstein has described the Tibetan region in the following terms: "there was a sort of national pilgrimage network in Tibet, whose routes, extending the length and breadth of the country, joined great and small temples and shrines, as well as caves, mountains, valleys and lakes that were imbued with sacred significance" (Kapstein, 2006, 238). The region of Rgyalrong can therefore be seen as part of this sacred geography in which land, rivers and mountains have spiritual significance for the people.

In marked contrast the current political regime looks at the region in purely materialistic terms. It is a resource to be used and exploited for the benefit of the nation of China as a whole. The mountains can provide rock and minerals and the rivers can provide hydro-electric power that is so much in demand by the eastern coastal cities of New China.

Rgyalrong Agriculture

The economy of Rgyalrong is dominated by subsistence agriculture. Three distinct ways of life can be seen in the Rgyalrong region: nomads of the grasslands, farmers of the river valleys and merchants and workers in the towns. The three are mutually interlinked. Many villages have traditionally controlled particular areas of grasslands on the high grounds above their valleys. The ancient *tusi* kingdoms expanded over the grasslands as their power and influence increased.

The towns are relatively modern and now have significant Han populations. Here the buildings are built of concrete in a style similar to that found in many Han towns in Sichuan. In the towns are located the Middle Schools where the children of the surrounding regions are expected to attend. Those who come from some distance board at the school from Monday to Friday.

Good agricultural land is very limited and so this becomes a major element in forming the way of life of the Rgyalrongwa. The nature of the terrain has meant that the Rgyalrong farmers have developed skills in cultivating the relatively dry river valleys. Apart from particular areas of the main valley caused by the meander of the river, there is little flat land suitable for cultivation. For this reason the farmers have made use of every available portion of land. This has often been achieved by terracing the land. Sometimes the terraces are quite extensive spreading over several kilometres, but usually the plots are small. The larger fields are divided between families, but the dividing line is not a wall or a fence, but a small flat stone placed at the middle of the space between two rows. The main problem with terraced fields is that the fields are small and require considerable maintenance. Terraced fields are therefore mainly cultivated by hand, which means much physical labour for the people.

Terraced fields near Badi

The land is generally fertile and has adequate rainfall. The climate allows a wide range of crops to be grown including barley, wheat, buckwheat, rye, potatoes and assorted fruits, vegetables and spices.

The planting time for wheat and corn are different in the main valley basin compared to the hills. Commonly, in the valley wheat is planted at the end of October and harvested on 1st June. Corn is planted 1st April and harvested in September. On the higher slopes, wheat is planted earlier, in mid-October and harvested in mid-June. Corn is planted in mid-April and harvested in September. Corn is generally planted in a warm sunny place and wheat in a cold place.

The most important crop in the Tibetan area is barley. The dough made from barley flour is called *tsampa*, which is notably the staple food on the grasslands. This is either rolled into noodles or made into steamed dumplings called *momos*. Meat dishes are likely to be yak, goat, or mutton, often dried, or cooked into a spicy stew with potatoes. Mustard seed is cultivated and features heavily in the cuisine.

Many different types of vegetables are grown in the Rgyalrong region - red and white carrots, beans, soya, peas, suancai and cabbage. Chilli peppers, peppercorn and garlic are grown to give spice to the dishes. There are also many fruits including green and red apples, plums, walnuts, oranges and melons. One often finds stores of barley, chillies, garlic and dried orange skins in the local houses.

Mixed cropping is a common practice to make maximum use of the fertile land. Corn and potatoes are often grown together. Once the potatoes have been collected, the leaves of the plant are removed to allow the corn to grow. As with all the cultivation in this area, it requires much backbreaking work as there is no alternative in the small plots on terraced slopes.

Yak yoghurt, butter and cheese are frequently eaten, and well-prepared yoghurt is considered something of a prestige item. Butter tea is a very popular drink and is served at every meal.

Animals

Unlike other domesticated animals, pigs are prized as sources of meat and little else. They can't be ridden, milked or used to pull or carry things. They are however the most efficient protein and fat producer of all domestic animals. Almost 35 percent of the food by weight fed to pigs is converted to meat, compared to only 13 percent for sheep. In the Tibetan region there is a different species of pig to that found in the plains of Sichuan. It is black in colour and is thinner than the normal species *Sus scrofa* (Yang et al., 2011). It therefore has a slightly different flavour, which some have seen as offering a marketing opportunity for the local people.

Pigs, together with a couple of cows, are commonly found in the animal pens on the ground floor of the houses. Although the animals may be allowed out to graze during the day they are brought back at night.

Grasslands

The Rgyalrongwa are not only farmers nor is their way of life merely located in the valleys. As already mentioned many of the families have areas of grassland on which they pasture some of their animals. The way of life of the people can therefore be seen as pastoral, agricultural and more recently urban.

The Tibetan Plateau consists of large areas of grassland out of which rocky mountains reach up to the "big sky" as it is called locally. In this high altitude environment, storms can quickly develop and snows cover the plateau for half of the year. Although sheep, cattle, goats and horses are pastured it is the yak that is the most distinctive animal of this unique environment.

The English word "yak" derives from the Tibetan (*g.yag*, or *gyag*). In Tibetan, this word refers only to the male of the species, while the female is called *dri* or *nak* (Singh, 2009). They are among the largest wild bovids. Wild male yak stand about 2 to 2.2 metres tall at the shoulder, can weigh 1,000 kg or more, and have a body length of 3 to 3.4 m. The females weigh about one third of this and are about 30% smaller in dimensions. Yaks are herd animals. Domesticated yaks however are much smaller, males weighing 350 to 580 kg and females 225 to 255 kg. Both sexes have long shaggy hair to insulate them from the cold. Wild yaks can be brown or black and, in addition, domesticated yaks can be white. Both male and female animals have horns.

Domestic yaks mate in about September. The females may first conceive at about 18 months of age, calving April to June, and can calve every year depending upon food supply. The gestation period is approximately 8.5 months. Calves will be weaned at one year and become independent shortly after. Yaks may live for more than 20 years. In the absence of more data, wild animals are assumed to follow this reproductive behaviour.

Domesticated yaks are kept primarily for their milk, hair, meat and as beasts of burden. Their dried dung is also an important fuel, used all over Tibet. It is often the only fuel available on the high treeless Tibetan plateau. Domestic cattle are crossbred with yaks, which gives rise to the infertile male *dzo* as well as fertile females known as *dzomo* or *zhom*. These may in turn be crossed again with cattle.

Yaks being moved by herder to winter pasture.

Like most nomadic herders there is a need for them to move their animals through the seasons. This transmigration is essential to allow the grass to grow in the difficult climatic environment. The animals are brought down from the higher grasslands during the winter season into the broad valleys of the plateau. The vast grasslands require the people to follow their traditional transhumance, but in recent years the Central Government has argued for the implementation of what has been called "scientific animal husbandry". In practice this has meant the fencing of animals into restricted areas. This has resulted in the grass becoming depleted and the average size of the animals has become smaller.

Foraging

Foraging for mushrooms and wild herbs is a common practice in the region. These are often used for Tibetan medicine. Roots, branches and stalks belong to a class of medicine that is collected in autumn (October–November) when the plants have become dry. These parts of the plants are said to be remedies for disorders of the bones, blood vessels, nerves and muscular tissue. Leaves and shoots belong to another class that are collected in mid-summer (June–July) when the plants are in their full growth. These parts of the plants are remedies for the disorders of the six hollow organs, bone marrow and cartilage. Flowers, fruits and tips belong to a third class that are collected in the autumn (August–September) when the plants begin to become yellow and fruits ripen. These parts of the plant are used for remedies for disorders on the sense organs and headaches (Thupten Phentsok & Tsewang Lhamo, 2009).

In the grasslands, there is another interesting growth that has become a significant source of income. From early May to mid-June, many people go to the highlands to look for *yartsa gunbu*, or "Caterpillar Fungus", an unusual creature that is half-plant and half-worm. It cannot be cultivated and grows thinly scattered and only on the high plateau. ("Yartsa Gunbu Cordyceps | Mushrooming - Daniel Winkler's Webpages Dedicated to Mushrooms and Nature Tours," n.d.). To collect this unusual species requires a lot of labour, but only simple equipment to collect.

The Tibetan name *yartsa gunbu* means "summer herb winter worm." The Chinese name is *chongcao*, meaning "insect grass", and goes by the Latin *Cordyceps Sinensis*. Wikipedia says that "caterpillar fungi are the result of a parasitic relationship between the [*cordyceps*] fungus and the larva of the ghost moth.... The fungus germinates in living organisms, and then the *cordyceps* grows from the body of the insect." In other words, the fungus invades the caterpillar, filling its entire body as it grows, killing the caterpillar and mummifying it. The fungus then grows out of the head of the caterpillar, continuing to grow until the fungus protrudes from the soil surface, a small brown finger reaching skyward. It releases its spores into the air and then it withers, still attached to the caterpillar. The two are conjoined as if they are one creature: half plant, half worm.

To find caterpillar fungus requires keen eyes as the fungus protrudes only two or three centimetres above the ground and is hidden among the vegetation. The best pickers are usually children aged 8–15 years. A good picker can harvest more than fifty worms a day. Customers for *Yartsa gunbu* are to be found in virtually every country of the world, the biggest markets being China and Japan where the worm is considered an important medicine. It is claimed that caterpillar fungus can be used to treat coughs, anaemia, tuberculosis, lower back pain, impotence, infertility, irregular menstruation, night sweats and senile weakness.

Generally, Tibetan pickers sell the worms to middlemen who come to towns like Kangding and Yushu in search of the product (Winkler, 2008). During the *yartsa gunbu* season, impromptu outdoor worm markets appear on city streets and bustle with activity as buyers and sellers haggle for the best prices. Sellers can also be found by the roadside waving bags of worms at passing traffic. Buyers transport the worms to major cities where the worms are cleaned, packaged, and distributed to retailers for sale. In late May, 2010 the Kangding market price averaged about $2.50/worm, but the cleaned product will sell for $60/worm in the city. For a family with many strong pickers, the income from *yartsa gunbu* can be substantial, upwards of 100,000 Yuan ($15,000) or more in the one-and-a-half month season. Because *yartsa gunbu* is extremely lucrative, worm-hunting territory is zealously guarded during collecting season by the community to which it belongs. With the stakes so high, fights over worm turf quickly turn violent.

Yartsa gunbu has brought something of an economic boom on the Tibetan plateau during the last ten years as demand has soared. The results are evident in the many motorcycles that have replaced horses as a transportation of choice. This has benefitted some of the people of Rgyalrong especially those living in the north of the region towards Amdo.

Problems

When talking to the Rgyalrong farmers about the problems they face several answers quickly come to the fore. One of the first relates to the land itself. Farm land is still owned and controlled by the state and is technically leased to farmers. This is a hangover from the commune era. Reforms passed in the time of Deng Xiao Ping allowed farmers a 30-year lease for the right to work a plot. Nevertheless, the local government can reclaim land and rezone it for non-agricultural use. The peasant-farmers have little say on the fate of the land though it may have been worked by their families for generations.

A policy approved by the Communist Party in October 2008, aimed at reducing rural poverty, gave farmers the right to trade, rent, sublet, sub-contract and transfer their land rights. This is beginning to help impoverished farmers and provide them with money they didn't have before, which should stimulate domestic spending and growth. This policy should be able to allow farmers to sell their produce more easily, but this raises a second problem for the farmers, which is that of transport. To sell their produce in the towns and cities, farmers need good roads for vehicles. Some of the villages in the smaller valleys are only accessible by minibuses, and so the produce has to be brought to the main road and then loaded onto larger trucks. All this involves more cost and logistic problems, which makes the task uneconomic. The only produce that is viable for many isolated villages is the caterpillar fungus mentioned earlier.

A third factor is the overall migration of the workforce from the land. This commences when children graduate from the village primary schools and move to the Middle schools in Danba, Kangding and Ma'erkang. Although children often return home for the weekends they are already becoming accustomed to life in the towns, and their education is geared to the national curriculum. Those who succeed at Middle school go on to colleges and universities, and they rarely want to return to the villages. As we have seen, farming requires much physical work and many young people do not want this, even though elderly parents may beg them to return to look after them and the land.

A fourth factor relates to environmental issues. In the 1970s and 1980s logging was an important way by which local people could make money, but it became evident that the loss of the trees was having a detrimental effect on the environment. The national government therefore banned logging in the region. Reforestation would help stabilize the environment, but there is little major effort being made in this respect.

The fifth and perhaps the most important issue facing the people of the valleys are the new hydroelectric projects that are being constructed. International reports speak of 23 cascade power stations along the Dadu valley (Berga, 2006, 22). In 2010, major projects were underway in Danba and Jinchuan, and several smaller ones such as in the narrow valley north of Badi.

The Hou Zi Yan dam is located 47 km downstream from Danba on the Dadu River. It has flooded an arid region that does not have much agricultural use and has slightly influenced the water height in Danba. It is reported that its capacity will be 1.76 Gigawatts, and the electricity will be transmitted to Chengdu and other places.

The Badi dam is located on the Da Jin Chuan River about 25 km upstream from Danba town. It will flood a region with some arable land, a monastery and some other items of tangible heritage. This dam will raise the water height in Danba, and should have a capacity of 1.14 Gigawatts.

The Danba dam is located on the Da Jin Chuan River about 2 km upstream from Danba town. It will also flood some arable land and raise the water in Danba. Its capacity is supposed to be 1.3 Gigawatts. The Jinchuan dam is located a few kilometres north of Danba.

Apart from the Hou Zi Yan, all these projects require the relocation of the local people from land that has been farmed by their family for generations. Although compensation is given by the local authorities, this is not sufficient to buy land in a region where there is little cultivatable land. The only option is that people have is to move to the towns and cities as migrant workers.

These massive building projects require the construction of new roads, bridges and power lines. In some cases, villages are drowned in the rising water, and in other cases longstanding neighbours are divided as the water spreads upstream. The construction work has polluted the river so that few fish are now seen, and there are frequent landslides (Jianping, Hongling, & Xinpo, 2006). Government slogans written on red banners over the sites remind the local people that this temporary inconvenience is for the good of the nation as a whole.

The sacred land is being redrawn by the massive technology of modern China. In spite of landslides, floods and bad roads the area is being changed. It will be several years before the long lakes that will be formed by the dams, and the new roads will have their effect. How will this effect tourism, which at one time was supposed to lift the local economy? Maybe better roads will help the famers in one way, but the loss of land will be a terrible tragedy to others.

4 Houses

It was the eminent anthropologist Lévi-Strauss who in a series of lectures at the College de France from 1976 through 1981 examined the concept of the 'house' in a survey of social organizations (Carstein, 1995). Those he chose ranged from the Canadian north-west coast through Indonesia, Melanesia, Polynesia, New Zealand, Madagascar and Micronesia. He introduced the concept of 'house' specifically to address problems encountered by ethnographers trying to classify societies according to their dominant kinship structure. In order to discuss 'house' in this social context he turned to Medieval Europe and modern Japan. He went on to speak about 'house societies' as a specific form of social organization. Lévi-Strauss' definition of a 'house' was that it is "a corporate body holding an estate made up of both material and immaterial wealth, which perpetuates itself through the transmission of its name, its goods and its titles down a real or imaginary line considered legitimate as long as this continuity can express itself in the language of kinship or of affinity and, most often, of both" (Levi-Strauss, 1982, 194). This model has been tested by various writers, most notably by those working in south-east Asia. One of the most important recent works is that by Roxana Waterson: *The living house* (Waterson, 2012).

In recent years anthropology has been increasingly used by architects to explore the context of what makes a house a home. A home can be seen as a technologically designed space to allow a family or community to meet specific individual and social needs. The approach to its design has drawn together the disciplines of architecture, anthropology and art. The houses of the minority peoples of Sichuan are quite distinct, and they change from area to area. Several scholars have recorded some of the changes in traditional Chinese styles of house (Berliner, 2012; Deqi Shan, 2011; Knapp, 2005) and Alexander has studied the changes in housing styles in Lhasa (Alexander, 2013).

The Villages

As previously mentioned, the valley of the Dadu River provides little flat land, so the people have made extensive use of terracing of the fields to maximize cultivation. For this reason the villages (乡 *xiang* or 村 *cun* in Chinese) tend to be compact even though the houses themselves are spacious. Often the steepness of hills means that there is no single area for the whole village, so the village consists of several small scattered hamlets.

With regards to cultural mapping in the region, roads and temples (with stupas) are the major features on the landscape. Roads and bridges tend to mark out the economic pathways in the region while the temples define the spiritual aspects. Until recently the major routes were no more than tracks. The famed "Tea Horse Trail" from Ya'an to Kangding and on to Lhasa was no more than a pathway sufficient for packhorses to pass along the river valley. The pathways up to the mountain villages were winding footpaths that zigzagged up the steep hillsides. Paths often ran along the sides of the hills connecting the mountain villages.

In the 1920s, a new kind of public road (*gong lu*) appeared connecting Ya'an and Tibetan areas to the west with Chengdu. Western-influenced urban planners and warlords throughout Sichuan championed road construction as a modernization priority. In 1935, the divisions of the Red Army passed through the region facing opposition from the local people along their journey. It was not until the 1960s that the roads were widened for motor traffic, but the flooding of the river and landslides frequently closed the region.

Today, many of the villages have a narrow single-track road that connects them to the main road that runs alongside the Dadu River. These minor roads have usually been cut into the steep face of the valley by the local villagers. These zigzag up the hillside with sharp hair-pin bends that require careful manoeuvring. Landslides following heavy rains are common and the repair of the road is an activity the village must be prepared for every year.

Single track road connecting a mountain village to the
main road running near the river in the valley.

Roads are important for any village as they provide access to the developments within the rest of China. For the villagers they allow access to markets and schools. For government officials they provide means by which taxes and government authority can be exercised. Villagers recognize these issues and are eager to help with the construction of roads from their mountain villages to the surfaced road that runs along the valley adjacent to the river. As John Flower writes:

> In contemporary China, road construction is a top priority
> for state economic planners as part of the effort to build
> "material civilization" (物质文明 *wuzhi wenming*). Roads,
> however, also invoke the discourse of "spiritual civilization" (

精神文明*jingshen wenming*) in that roads can transport the "peasant" out of his backward conservatism by integrating him with a progressive global economy. The civilizing mission of road construction creates an emerging border–physical and conceptual–between the new cosmopolitan China and its backward hinterland (Flower, 2004).

Due to the lie of the land and zenith of the Sun, houses in a village often have a common orientation. The houses are usually built with a veranda on the third floor positioned so as to catch the warmth of the afternoon and evening sunshine. Thus, looking over a village the houses appear as forming a matrix structure with each house having the same general orientation. Narrow lanes only 2 or 3 meters in width cross the village allowing access for people and animals.

The village of Qiong Shan, Badi illustrates the common orientation of the houses.

In previous times the senior families may have had a tower close to or attached to their houses. These towers have fascinated scholars for many years and discussions continue as to the nature of their primary function. This distinctive architectural feature will be discussed in the following chapter.

In the Danba-Badi area many of the older houses were constructed around the tower. The tower was first built on a suitable rock and this was used to set the shape of the house. When the houses are demolished by the local people in order to use the wood or timber, it is noteworthy that the towers are left standing. The local people regard these towers as "the spirit of the family" which should be preserved. In Badi four houses were badly damaged by a flash-flood, and eventually the houses were dismantled for the stone and wood. The towers that were the basis of the construction could then be clearly seen.

House Design

Like houses everywhere in rural China, the Rgyalrong houses are second only to land as a means of material production. They provide the setting for innumerable tasks that depend on different conditions of light, heat and moisture (UNESCO, 2013). The orientation to the sun, the location of cooking stoves, the direction of drainage and overhanging eaves all produce distinctive environments. The eaves and roof of the house create dry, sunny places where people can work and hemp and foodstuff can dry. The shady north side produces cool, damp places where straw and manure can decompose slowly into compost and where vegetables are kept fresh. There are dry and dark places where grain would only lose its moisture slowly, and smoky places where meat would not rot. Rgyalrong houses have therefore been shaped to provide an effective centre for material production.

Rgyalrong houses have a common design consisting of 3 or 4 floors with a rectangular plan. The thick walls are constructed from carefully placed large stones with smaller ones filling the gaps. Careful use of a plumb line ensures stability and safety to the structure. The stones are held together with mortar made from mud, which allows the surface of the wall to become reasonably smooth. Today the walls are coated with cement both on the inside and outside.

As a result of increasing deforestation, the Chinese government enforced a total ban on logging in the region as of 1st September 1999. One impact of the ban has been a shortage of building materials, since the gathering of timbers has traditionally been the responsibility of the homeowner or the monastery. In response to this, the government has stated that individuals will still be permitted access to these resources upon receipt of a special permit (Semple, 2005).

Thick wooden trunks are embedded into the walls to form the floors. These are set to pass through the wall and on the outside a wooden plank is fixed, which provides not only decoration but often a means of access to the outside. Across these beams lighter wood is placed, and small stones are spread to fill the gaps and provide a level surface. The floor is then finally cemented to provide a smooth surface to the flooring.

Wooden beams are also used to construct the windows. Traditionally the windows were small with wooden shutters to provide protection from the chill wind and possible attackers. They also allow an exit for the smoke from the fire, but this still does not take way the impact of the smoke on the eyes when one enters the kitchen. Today, windows are being made larger with the use of glass.

The first (or ground) floor of the house is essentially a storage area and a pen for the animals. The storage areas are under the main rooms on the upper floor, while the animal pens are generally uncovered apart from a small area where the animals can shelter from the rain. These storage areas are not very high, but adequate for the purpose. It is usually possible to look down from the second and third floors into the animal pen. A small door in the wall of the pen itself allows a way for the animals to be taken out of the pen into the narrow lanes and out to the fields to graze.

The second floor consists of the kitchen and dining areas as well as the stairway up to the third floor. As so much of the land is on the side of the valley, frequently the house is constructed so that the main entrance is at the higher side. This means one enters at the second floor possibly after a few steps. The second floor is the centre of activity with food preparation and dining. It is here that the family gathers on a cold evening to sit around the central fire to tell stories of the day's activities.

Traditional kitchen with central fire

The third floor is the main sleeping area, but as mentioned earlier a large area provides a south facing veranda. Here the family can work in the warmth of the sunshine, dry their corn and other crops and entertain visitors. There is usually a low wall around the veranda that provides a convenient sitting area and in addition offers some security against the two-storeyed drop into the animal pen. This is particularly so because the walls are capped with flat stones to stop the rain entering into the wall and these make convenient seats.

The fourth floor, which is essentially the roof of the house, is flat with more area to sit in the sunshine. There is a slight gradient to the surface so that the water can drain off through drainage holes. It is on this floor that there is often a shrine room and a small chimney. The chimney is usually built into the side of the house and it is here that the oldest male member of the household will burn dry twigs and moss to produce a white smoke that rises high into the sky to the home of the gods. The subject of the shrine room will be returned to later.

The steps leading from the different floors were traditionally made of tree trunks into which notches have been cut to provide footholds. The art of scaling these initially seems daunting to the western visitor, but family members climb with little difficulty. Nevertheless, today metal steps are being introduced for added convenience.

The toilet facility is usually on the north side of the house on the second and third floors. This consists of a wooden structure that projects out from the wall; privacy is provided by a wooden fence. Shelter is given by a sloping roof, and a slot in the floor provides a passage through which excrement falls into the pit below. The excrement is later collected and provides useful fertilizer for the soil.

The walls of the house are painted white apart from a strip along the roof of the house which is red or dark brown. This colour is also used around the windows. Another strip is often painted below the brown around the roof, and this is a black and white pattern that can vary from village to village.

A spiritual castle

So far we have discussed the material structure of a typical Rgyalrong house, but there is also a spiritual dimension that has already been alluded to. This is seen both in the intrinsic design and in the dedication of the building such that the house becomes a place of spiritual protection for the family. The deities are incorporated into the very construction of the house making it in effect a castle (*dzongka*) against the malevolent forces outside. The average Tibetan house would have a number of "houses" or "seats" (*poe-khang*) for the male god (*pho-lha*) who protects the house. Every day the eldest male of the house would invoke this god and burn juniper wood and leaves to placate him. In addition the woman of the house would also have a protecting deity (*phuk-lha*) whose seat can be found within the kitchen usually at the top of the pole that supports the roof.

The dedication of the house takes place after the walls and floors have been constructed and the family is able to live in the property. The walls may need to be faced with cement and painted, but that can be done later. On the day of dedication friends and family are invited to the house to socialize, play cards, eat and take part in the religious activities. The major part of dedication consists of chanting from the Bön sutras, which is led by the local Bön shaman who presides over the ritual. The local monk or lama (dGelug, 'Yellow hat") may also attend, but this is more a matter of respect and hospitality rather than to participate in the ritual. If the family have converted to dGelug tradition the monks will take a more significant role.

There are two elements of the design that are particularly significant. The first relates to the roof of the house where 'horns' are constructed at the corners. These are made by sloping the wall upward about one metre, so that this meets in a peak at the corners. This peak is capped with a flat stone on which is placed a large white stone known as *labtse* (*la-btsas*) or *mudo* (*dmu-rdo*). Sometimes these are ordinary stones that have been painted white, but always there is a white stone known as the spirit of the stone *(guoguo sheng)*. It is onto the horns that coloured flags are set up to blow in the wind to bring blessing to the family. The choice of colour is usually divined by the shaman as that which will be most auspicious for the family for the coming year.

The horns give the Rgyalrong house one of its most characteristic features. The neighbouring Qiang people are particularly known for their veneration of the white-stone (Graham, 1958:50). Although among the Rgyalrong it is not seen as worship, it is seen as having an important spiritual dimension. Beneath the horns of the house are placed wooden gargoyles usually having the appearance of a dragon. For a new house, this stands out with its bright colours and strong shape. However, its location means it is exposed to the weather and so can quickly deteriorate, and for this reason a flat stone is placed on top of the gargoyle to provide some protection.

The top storey of this integrated structure is known as a *choekhang* (*chos-khang*), and is where the household and territorial deities are propitiated. These shrine rooms are only 3 or 4 metres in size. On the far end is an altar on which offerings of water and fruit are made daily. Brightly coloured thangkas are hung on the side walls. This is the place where a visiting monk would be invited to stay, and rituals of blessing for the family performed as the following photograph shows.

Shaman at work in the shrine room

Another important feature of the house design is the doorway. As with many societies, doorways are where the intimacies of the living space come in contact with the imagined universe. They allow the inner and outer spaces contact and are therefore considered places of potential danger and so need special spiritual protection. The Rgyalrongwa, like many Chinese people, have a wooden step across the entrance of the outermost doors. Sometimes the door is quite low so that a person has to bow their head to enter. Thus, when an enemy enters he will be vulnerable at that moment. One folk superstition says that a zombie (the living dead) will not be able to enter because they can't bend at the waist.

On either side of the door Chinese characters written on red paper are hung to bring blessing on all who enter. These writings are replaced every year or at some special event. Above the main door two carved wooden dragons peer out and above them is often placed a picture of a great bodhisattva. Various items can be placed around the doorway both to offer protection and to express the hope of an abundant provision for the household. The items chosen depend on the choice of the particular family or more often the advice of the shaman. For example, in one house I observed a wood saw hung above the door as a symbol of protection, and strings of corn cobs and red peppers hanging at the sides of the door to signify an ample supply of food.

Changes in design

Ewing is one of the few writers who has discussed the changes in architectural style in the Kham area of Eastern Tibet (Ewing, 2003). In recent years there has been a steady change in the basic facilities and contents of the houses.

New house being built in Badi.

Initially it was the arrival of tools and other items that were mass produced in the cities and could be sold cheaply in the local towns. Plastic buckets and aluminium pots replaced the traditional clay posts.

There are many skilled local carpenters in the region, employed to build houses and to work on the construction and restoration of temples and monasteries. But the amount of work available for local carpenters has been steadily decreasing, compounded by the influence of Chinese modernism and the dogma, which now dominates national policy, that "modernism and science" are a solution to all problems. Traditional ways of life and knowledge are overlooked to the extent that carpenters in rural areas often view the new glass and concrete buildings as something superior, with their own ideas being primitive. (Semple, 2005)

It was the coming of electricity that made one of the major changes to the lives of the people. This has not only allowed electric lights, but for those who had the wealth, the possibility to acquire televisions, DVD players and even refrigerators. Today nearly all the houses have a satellite dish positioned on the top of the house. The geography of the region may reduce the number of channels, but television provides closer contact with the outside world. Cheap CDs and DVDs are available in the towns and these add to the entertainment for the families.

Water is another important facility and families have bought blue plastic piping to bring water from the streams into their homes. The local government has sometimes offered free piping to encourage villages to install a clean water supply. Since 2000, some families have also started making use of solar power with water running through panels on the roof. The bright sunshine at these high altitudes means that the solar heaters provide a good supply of hot water for the family. Curved metal sheets have also been fabricated to focus the sunlight onto a cooking pot in order to heat water or cook food. These are good examples of applied development.

Most of the houses were built decades or even centuries ago, and have been repaired and extended over the years. More recently those families with sufficient money have begun to totally rebuild their houses, and one of the major changes is the separation of the animals from the immediate vicinity of the house. The government has encouraged this as the smell brings flies and along with them disease. Another reason for this change has been the development of tourism in the area as will be discussed in chapter 14.

5 Towers

One of the most fascinating aspects of Rgyalrong architecture is the stone towers. These have been studied for many years by the French explorer, Frederique Darragon (Darragon, 2006). She has done much to bring these amazing buildings to the knowledge of the international community and is seeking to have them listed as having UNESCO World Heritage status. Rammed-earth and wood towers that have various architectural styles are found in many parts of China especially the well-known Kaiping towers in the south of the country (Cheng Yu Wai, 2003). Stone towers are only found in the "tribal corridor" and especially among the Rgyalrong and the neighbouring Qiang people.

In recent years, the most accessible towers have become tourist attractions for visitors from wealthier areas of China and even some international tourists (Yang Jiaming, 2004). Those towers in more isolated locations can only be found with some difficulty and often there is little left to see other than a pile of stones. Darragon has done excellent work locating many of these derelict towers and fixing the location by means of GPS.

Design of the Towers

Darragon distinguishes the freestanding towers as having two main designs (Darragon, 2009). The first is a square shape with a square interior space, which she considers to be the most common. The second is what Darragon calls "star-shape". These often have eight-corners (16-sides) with a circular inner space. Some may have as many as

13-corners, but they still have a circular inner space. Such a star-shape design is particularly rare throughout the world, and examples have only been found in parts of Iran, Tajikistan, Afghanistan and Chechnya. The Nakh people of Chechnya are known to have built square towers for military purpose for many centuries. ("Nakh architecture," 2013). Although agreeing with many of Darragon's points, I have seen that many towers have a basic square inner space irrespective of their outward shape. Some are merely square-shaped towers with corners sticking out from the middle of each side, which gives an overall eight-cornered shape. There are also many towers that are part of the very structure of a house or palace, which will be discussed later.

In addition to these general comments, the towers have certain similar characteristics. First, their outer walls slope slightly inwards making the base larger in area than the top. This lowers the centre of gravity and makes the overall structure more stable. This is particularly important as this region is often subject to earthquakes such as in May 2008 and April 2013.

The Rgyalrong towers are made of uncut stones of varying sizes held together with mortar made of a soil and clay mixture. The modern style of cement is only recently available and so was never previously used to construct towers. Near Wenchuan, in a Qiang area, there are multi-storey towers made of beaten-earth, but none of these have been found among the Rgyalrong. Large wooden beams are embedded into the walls with smaller beams crossing at right-angles in order to provide a viable floor. Wooden ladders made by cutting notches into the trunk of a small tree allow access to the different floors. The beauty of this design is that the ladder can easily be lifted up floor-by-floor as the person ascends the tower.

What also provides clues as to the purpose of the towers are the entrances, or lack of them. First, many of the square towers are built next to, or as part of, a three-storey house. Here access is only made from the house itself via the top floor. Local people tell that many of these towers were destroyed during the Cultural Revolution (1967-77). In recent years some houses have rebuilt low towers, which the people say adds prestige to the house. Local authorities are taking up this style when building tourist facilities in the region as it adds a distinctive character that is sought by tourists.

Second, some of the free-standing towers are only accessed by having to go through an underground passage before one can enter by a small door. This type of entrance has become filled in over the years so that they are not immediately obvious. The aim of this design seems to have been that when under attack these entrances could be filled to make hostile entry extremely difficult. Those inside could exit and enter by means of a rope lowered down from a window on the third or fourth floor, or by a ladder to a neighbouring roof as shown in the following figure. It is said some towers even had a small passage going underground from the base of the tower to some hidden exit point many metres away.

Exiting from a freestanding block tower onto the roof of an adjacent house.

Third, the tops of the Qiang towers are different from those of the Rgyalrong in that the latter are flat while those of the Qiang have a covered access. This single-storey walled room that covers the access on the roof gives the top of the Qiang tower the appearance of a step, which has become a characteristic of their towers. This cover is usually on the north-side of the tower, which means the top of the tower catches the sunshine and is protected from the north winds. In contrast, the Rgyalrong tower is flat consisting of a wall around the beaten-earth of the top floor. Local builders tell about the special mixture they use for the flat roof that consists of up to 10 ingredients. One of these is the waxy resin from pine trees, which would obviously give the surface good waterproofing properties. There are also wooden pipes set into the walls so that rain water runs off the roof and away from the building itself.

Dating the construction of the towers

Before returning to the question of the function of the towers, it is necessary to consider the dates when the towers were built. Darragon has approached this question in two ways. The first is by referring to the ancient Chinese records and the second is by the use of modern carbon dating techniques.

Towers in a square design are mentioned in Chinese records from the Han dynasty (206 BC to 210 AD). The Chinese words used were *Diao* 碉, *Diaofang* 碉房 and *Diaolou* 碉楼. These words are those currently used for the traditional Tibetan multi-storeyed stone-built house. As Darragon notes, these houses have a defensive connotation by the very nature of their construction, but it would be wrong to extend the words used in these ancient texts to mean a tall tower. In Chinese, a defensive tower would probably have been called a *Ditai* (敌台).

The star-shaped towers are first mentioned in the sixteenth century during the Ming Dynasty (Darragon, 2006). This suggests that until this time few, or no Chinese people had seen star-shaped towers. In 1944, Deng Shaoqin wrote about the legend of She Wu and the "Xixia

Kingdom". Although, the whole study was discounted by R.A. Stein, because Deng Shaoqin only wrote of what he heard, in the eighth chapter he provides a list of locations of star-shaped towers (Stein, 1972). Darragon has found this list to be quite accurate, even if limited, and this enabled her to locate some towers.

Scholars generally agree that many towers were built during the 18th century. As was mentioned in chapter 2, the eighteen or so *Tusi* (local kings) built defensive structures that enabled them to successfully resist the armies of Emperor Qianglong during the First Jinchuan War. Darragon has found that none of the towers that she has dated are that recent. She therefore concludes that these 18th century towers must have been destroyed during the Second Jinchuan War that saw the Emperor's armies victorious through the use of cannons built and directed by the Jesuits in the service of the Emperor.

The second method of dating the towers is by carbon dating. (Darragon, 2008; Scharf, A, 2013). The moment an organism dies it stops taking up carbon, and so the minute amounts of the radioactive Carbon 14 begin to decay. Carbon 14 has a half-life of 5,730 years and so scholars consider this method of dating is accurate up to 60,000 years (plus or minus 1%). It can give a dating with an accuracy of plus or minus 50 years if less than 5,000 years.

The main problem however is finding a sample of wood from a tree that was cut down at the same time that the tower was constructed. Large beams are valuable items and so are stored and reused if still sound, or smaller portions are cut from the original if there has been damage. Collecting wood samples is therefore very difficult. In many towers, all that is left are broken beams often out of reach without a tall ladder. If many beams of the same towers can be dated, the results are more trustworthy, but carbon dating is expensive. Darragon usually tried to cut samples from small beams because she assumes these were unlikely to have been cut long before the construction in which they were used.

The first two samples that she sent for analysis in the year 2000 gave an age of 650 years for a tower in Kongpo and the west twin Tower of Remede was dated from 1038 to 1274 AD. The oldest wood sample she has dated was more than 1700 years old, but most of the samples were around 700 years old. The oldest tower she found was not in the Rgyalrong area at all, but hundreds of kilometres away in the Tibetan Autonomous Region in what would have been the period of the ancient kingdom of Nyango, which corresponds to modern Gongbu Jiangda Xian.

Although the study shows that such tall towers have been built in the region for many hundreds of years, it does not prove the existing towers are as ancient as the wood samples. As already mentioned, wood and stones are frequently reused by the people, and this is true even today. I have seen wooden beams being dug out of houses destroyed in the earthquake in 2008 to be used in new buildings. If a tower collapses it is quite likely that the stone and wood will be reused to construct another building. Large wooden beams are a rare resource in the area and take time and effort to prepare, so they are of great value.

When we talk about these towers, we should not therefore think that we are dealing with ancient structures like the pyramids of Egypt or the Parthenon in Athens. The towers may best be regarded as a particular building style characteristic to this mountainous region and a distinctive expression of the culture of the people.

Purpose of the Towers

When asking the local people about the origins and function of the towers, one never receives a definite answer, but only guesses or suggestions passed on from the older generation. A common explanation is that they were watch towers, and this is how the towers are often described in English today. With the increasing number of tourists asking the same question the local people tend to find this the simplest answer to satisfy the curious visitors. Scholars however have made more detailed suggestions.

The first suggestion already referred to is that they were indeed watchtowers for defensive purposes. This was certainly the case for those towers built during the eighteenth century when they proved to be a real hindrance to the Qing army during the Jinchuan Wars. The Qing could not easily breach the strong towers, but eventually some of the villagers explained how the local resistance fighters got food and water through underground passages. Armed with this information, the Qing forces poisoned the water supplies to the towers so that the defenders died, and the Qing soldiers were able to conquer the Rgyalrong area. After the defeat of the Rgyalrong, not only were some of the towers demolished, but some of the Rgyalrong soldiers were taken to Beijing to instruct the Chinese in this form of warfare.

The towers, however, should not be thought of as a form of castle into which villagers ran for protection. The internal design of the existing towers has only limited space allowing only 6, or at the most 10 men to move about freely. There are also only a few small windows, which not only means the ventilation is poor, but they are of limited value for shooting arrows. It would also have been very easy for the defenders to become trapped within the towers by fire or smoke, and underground escape tunnels would have been necessary.

A second associated theory was proposed by Eric Mortensen (a Tibetan scholar at the National Taiwan University) is that they were signal towers. This is a likely suggestion as the tops of many of the towers provide a clear line of sight from one to another, so messages could easily have been transmitted along the towers. However, this is not the full answer as there are many sites having a cluster of towers where only one would have been necessary for this purpose.

Thirdly, the towers could also have been markers along the valley indicating the location of the villages in a similar way to church steeples in medieval Europe. Most of the valleys are situated on the *Cha Ma Gu Dao* ("Tea and horse trail"), which was one of the ancient trading routes. The towers could possibly have indicated places where water, food and shelter were available for people and animals. Towers are not only found near houses, but sometimes are located on isolated ridges. This would suggest they could have acted as markers between territories, or even taxation points for the *tusi* wanting to profit from passing traders. However, this moves us into the area of speculation until further evidence is discovered.

Fourth, the towers may have been a status symbol for the king and local community. Most of the royal palaces had such a tower as part of the inherent structure of the palace building or freestanding nearby. Once a tower was constructed it would certainly have given status to the household and community. In the area of Badi it is said that if you adopt a son you must promise to build a tower. Every following year one storey is built until it reaches 13 storeys when the boy is regarded as being an adult.

A fifth reason that has been proposed for their construction is that they had a religious significance. As mentioned previously, the original Bön tradition of the region is based on animism and shamanism. In shamanic traditions there is a concept of an *axis muni*—a central column by which the shaman can rise to the higher realms and travel on his "power animal" to achieve healing (Eliade, 1991). Sacred trees are often seen as symbolizing this function, and some scholars have suggested this function for the Rgyalrong towers.

Darragon tells of Sherab Lekden, a monk resident at the Bön monastery situated above the town of Ma'erkang (Bellezza, 2009). He and some other Bönpa monks believe that even the most ancient towers in the region (founded no later than the 12th century AD) were originally particularly constructed as places where personal and territorial deities were worshipped. The burning of incense is said to have constituted the most common ritual practice. Some of these ancient ritual structures are six-sided or star-shaped. The religious or ceremonial function of the Rgyalrong towers is borne out by their geographic positions, although a good proportion of them occupy high slopes and ridgelines that possess very little inherent strategic value. These towers are usually isolated structures, not walled in or appended to other defensive structures. Consequently, they are vulnerable to the siege tactics of a determined enemy.

As was suggested in the previous chapter, the traditional domestic architecture of Rgyalrong supports the view that the ancient towers had a religious/ceremonial function. The houses of the region include turrets that are three and sometimes four storeys tall. The top storey of this integrated structure is known as a *choekhang* (*chos-khang*), and is where the household and territorial deities are propitiated (although many households now have a shrine room within the main body of the house, as is customary in most places in Tibet). The rooftop shrines are surmounted by white stones known as *lattés*(*la-btsas*) or *mudo* (*dmu-rdo*). The free-standing ancient towers appear to be the direct architectural predecessors of the domestic turrets. When the ancient towers are surveyed, investigators should search for traces of the divine white stones as their presence would confirm their religious function.

Darragon has proposed the following hypothesis regarding the origins of the towers. Commencing with the suggestion that the Rgyalrong originated from ancient Zhang-zhung, as was mentioned in chapter 2, it is known that they had a pantheon of celestial deities. The towers of Rgyalrong could therefore have been constructed in an attempt to express the skyward aspect of the grasslands. The word for the firmament in Rgyalrong language is *dmu*, which is also a class of sky deities. This seems to support the idea that the ancient towers did indeed have celestial connotations, but the star-shaped towers have never been mentioned in any religious book. Samten Karmay, a native from Rgyalrong and now a researcher at the CNRS in Paris, totally rejects the theory that the towers have any religious purpose.

An associated purpose for the towers that some local people have suggested to me is that the towers were built to protect the village from bad feng-shui. Towers are sometimes located between the village and the river such that they could act as a barrier to repeal bad feng-shui. Stupas are often found in similar locations. Careful cultural mapping would be needed to further explore this suggestion.

While the debate continues, it seems more than likely that the towers had various functions that changed with time. The earliest towers may well have had a ritual function as well as being one of status for the king (queen) or household. Those towers built as part of a house or palace would also have a practical function for storage as well as status. Later towers may have had a military function as it is known that the Rgyalrongwa used the towers for small armed encounters, particularly during 18th century battles against the Manchus. The strategically placed slits in the walls on the roofs give a clear line of sight to attackers coming along a road or across a bridge.

Today the towers have taken on another function which is that of a tourist attraction. In places near to major roads the towers have been rebuilt and near them new tourist accommodation has been created as in Suopo near the town of Danba.

Conservation

Scholars from the University of Rome have made a study of the effects of environmental vibration on the towers (Vergata, 2008). The main problems as they saw were decay in the quality of the masonry, changing conditions of the soil and foundation, structural instability and vulnerability to temporary loads.

My studies would suggest that there are two major effects that are observable. First, many of the towers show signs of crumbling at the top resulting in some of the masonry falling away.

Tower broken at the top

With time, more and more of the masonry breaks away and the tower slowly loses height. This often commences on the south facing wall of the tower, which in the winter months especially can experience marked daily changes in temperature. At noon the sun is directly onto the south face making the surface quite hot to the touch, while the north side, which is in the shade, remains cold and even icy. During the night the temperature drops well below zero. This marked temperature change on the south side could cause the clay that binds the stones to degenerate so they begin to slide out of position. The resultant wedge shaped top is then open to the environment and increasing degradation.

The second problem occurs when the foundation of the tower begins to lean due to the instability of the soil. When I pointed out a tower that was beginning to lean, the headman of Suopo readily provided the following explanation. The tower was next to a house while on the other side were cultivated fields. The soil around the house was trampled down hard so that the surface water readily drains away. In contrast each year the field was ploughed and watered so that the soil was soft and water could permeate under the foundations. This meant that the foundations on the side away from the house have begun to sink so that the tower has started to lean. All the local people were aware that eventually the tower would collapse and fall away from the house when there is an earthquake or strong wind, and so everyone avoids the area immediately to that side of the tower. This is a very reasonable explanation, which shows not only an understanding of the structure of their buildings, but an acceptance that towers are not seen to be permanent structures. Once buildings collapse the stones and wood are quickly taken by people to build new structures.

Towers at Suopo: one is beginning to lean.

Another issue raised by the team from the University of Rome is the damage that could be caused by uncontrolled tourism. In addition, the loss of heritage resources may be due to physical deterioration caused by inadequate maintenance or by simple neglect. Tourism could provide funding for the preservation of this interesting area rich in cultural and historical elements. In addition, as the local authorities realize, tourism can revitalize the economy of the whole area, generating employment opportunities and improving the way of life of the community. From a social point of view, as will be discussed in chapter 14, tourism can also encourage the revival of traditions, promote the preservation of their culture, enhance the sense of identity of the community and promote cultural exchange.

Intensive tourism development can have a negative impact both on the environment and the local inhabitants. A sustainable approach should move in the direction of increasing tourism benefits and decreasing negative effects. A careful feasibility study must evaluate whether and how tourism can be developed. Without sustainable oriented management, tourism loses its potential for growth.

The Rome University project proposed some strategies to help achieve sustainability. (Vergata, T. 2008). These strategies are here reviewed in the light of the current study and recent changes in the region. The following suggestions aim to try and preserve the distinctive architectural feature of the Rgyalrong in a way that is sustainable, will protect the environment and will provide some long-term employment for the local population.

First, any new buildings that are constructed should not be of a totally different style. When new buildings are constructed every effort should be made to promote environmental sensitivity by using local materials, and making designs compatible with existing buildings. The focus should be on conservation and rehabilitation of existing structures.

Second, large tourist settlements should be avoided in preference for small resorts in the heart of the existing community. This will not only give tourists a better experience the way of life of the local people, but will give them a greater sense of authenticity, which they so often seek.

Third, every effort should be made to promote the use of renewable energy. Sustainability requires that human activity only uses resources at a rate at which they can be replenished naturally. Reforestation of some of the region would be an important dimension for sustainability.

Four, there should be information available to the community concerning the importance of local cultural heritage. The local people should be actively involved in the decisions concerning tourism, and should have relevant education that enables them to make informed decisions. This education should commence with the children in Primary Schools and continue through all age groups. This theme will be taken up again in chapter 15 that will discuss education in the area.

6 Arts and Crafts

Scholars have often discussed the difference between a craft and an art. In the Oxford On-line Dictionary craft is defined as "an occupation or trade requiring manual dexterity" whereas art is defined as "works to be appreciated primarily for their beauty or emotional power." These definitions suggest that a craft is a production process whilst an art is the product of creativity and imagination. Crafts are therefore often portrayed as something more primitive, utilitarian and for everyday use. These items include pottery, textiles, and wood carvings among other things. Art, in contrast is considered to be more refined and sophisticated and is appreciated for its intrinsic beauty (Markowitz, 1994).

When a small-scale society comes in contact with a dominant civilization the advanced technology of the larger society has a major impact upon the local arts and crafts. This is because arts and crafts are the product of their social, political, and economic contexts of production; changing this context means changing the product. Over the centuries Chinese luxury goods have always been prized among the minority peoples of western China, but locally produced items remained the major items for most ordinary purposes. During the last century, however, cheap mass produced plastic and metal pots entered the markets of these minority communities. These vessels and containers were cheaper and more durable than those traditionally made, and so they have come to dominate the mass market. Local crafts have therefore been marginalized either to the cheapest of products or to become specialist hand-made products. In other words, just because a production method formerly yielded a craft item this does not mean that it will only ever yield a craft item, but it may produce something regarded as a work of fine art.

This process can be seen in the cultural changes that have occurred among the Rgyalrongwa during the twentieth century. The result has been that many of the traditional crafts are no longer economically viable, and the skills do not seem worthwhile passing onto the children. The young people likewise do not see the value of learning skills that will not eventually provide a livelihood. In such a situation it is possible for all the traditional crafts to be quickly lost from within a community. People only know that these crafts were once practiced, but now the skills have been lost. These skills are the "intangible heritage" of the people, and they are dying out in many parts of China even though the Central government is seeking to revitalize them. ("中国非物质文化遗产网," 2006).

Cultural heritage ("national heritage" or just "heritage") is the legacy of physical artefacts and intangible attributes of a community that are inherited from previous generations, maintained in the present and then bestowed for the benefit of future generations. Cultural heritage includes tangible culture (such as buildings, monuments, landscapes, books, works of art and artefacts), intangible culture (such as folklore, traditions, language and knowledge), and natural heritage (including culturally–significant landscapes and biodiversity).

On October 17th, 2003 UNESCO passed a resolution named *Convention for the Safeguarding of the Intangible Cultural Heritage*. The Convention identifies five broad domains: 1) Oral traditions and expressions—language being the vehicle, 2) Performing arts, 3) Social practices, rituals and festive events, 4) Knowledge and practices concerning nature and the universe, and 5) Traditional craftsmanship.

Lowenthal states that preserved objects validate memories (Lowenthal, 1994). While digital acquisition techniques can provide a technological record of the appearance of artefacts, the object itself as opposed to a reproduction, draws people in and gives them a literal way of touching the past. This unfortunately poses a danger as places and things are damaged by the hands of tourists, the light required to display them, and other risks of making an object known and available. The reality of this risk reinforces the fact that all artefacts are in a constant state of chemical transformation, so that what is considered to be preserved is actually changing—it is never as it once was. Similarly changing is the value each generation may place on the past and on the artefacts that link it to the past.

Thangka painting

Thangka (or Tangka, thanka or tanka) painting has become synonymous with Tibetan art. One of the most famous areas where Thangka are still being painted by local artists is Kandze, in the west of Sichuan province. Here the culture department established the Thangka Research Institute (*Zanghua Yanjiuyuan*) in 1986-7. The first exhibition of thangkas was organized in the spring of 2000. The exhibition revealed a great interest among the general public. In 2007 Chengdu hosted the first international exhibition of Intangible Heritage in which Thangka painting was highlighted.

Thangkas perform several different functions. The images of deities are important teaching tools depicting the life (or lives) of the Buddha, describing historical events concerning important Lamas, and retelling myths associated with other deities. Devotional images can act as the centrepiece during a ceremony and are often used as mediums through which prayers can be offered. Perhaps most importantly thangkas are used as a tool for meditation to help the devotee to travel further on the path to enlightenment.

Thangkas are usually painted on cotton or silk. The most common is loosely woven cotton produced in widths from 40 to 58 centimetres (16 – 23 inches). The paint consists of pigments in a water soluble medium. Both mineral and organic pigments are used, tempered with a herb and glue solution.

The composition of a thangka, as with the majority of Buddhist art, is highly geometric. Arms, legs, eyes, nostrils, ears, and various ritual implements are all laid out on a systematic grid of angles and intersecting lines. A skilled thangka artist will generally select from a variety of predesigned items to include in the composition, ranging from alms bowls and animals, to the shape, size, and angle of a figure's eyes, nose, and lips (Kværne, 1995). The process seems very methodical, but often requires deep understanding of the symbolism involved to capture the spirit of it. In the chapter discussing the conservation of the New Year Festival in Badi, a new thangka was produced of the "hero" who defeated the forces of evil.

In recent years the Rgyalrong area has been increasingly influenced by Kandez and Lhasa style of Thangka painting. This is seen in the way that the interior of rooms and furniture are now being painted. One of the reasons for this is that this brighter style has become associated in the minds of the Han Chinese and perhaps with the Rgyalrongwa themselves as being genuine Tibetan culture.

Seat in Badi being painted in "Lhasa style".

In an attempt to preserve some of these skills among the Rgyalrong, the Institute of Education at Sichuan Normal University, Chengdu sought to identify craftsmen in the region. Most of these people were in their 70s, and had come to regard their craft as out-of-date and of little use. One exception was that of sewing and embroidery done by the women. This is a pastime that has been communicated from mother to daughter for generations. However, even here when girls go to Middle School in the towns there is less time for them to learn these skills.

The project attempted both to record the traditional skills of these crafts people and to encourage some younger people to learn these skills before the skills died with the elders. To achieve these, both the crafts person and his apprentices were given payment for the time they spent in teaching or learning the skill. This was seen as a form of vocational education that may provide some local people new skills that could generate income through the production of traditional items that could be sold as souvenirs to tourists.

Black Pottery

One of the first crafts studied was "black pottery", which had been produced in the area for many centuries. In the central part of the Rgyalrong region one elderly man was discovered who knew how the pots had been made in the past. The project invited him to train four local men in this skill.

Black pottery was known in ancient Greece, India and in China for centuries. Initially the pots were made by coiling the clay into ropes and then carefully smoothed using a paddle on the exterior pressed against an anvil on the inside wall. Later, the potter's wheel was invented, the kiln was improved, and so the production of pottery made a great leap forward. The Longshan Black Pottery of China reached a peak in its quality more than 4,000 years ago when the black colour was produced by making black smoke at the end of the firing process. Today, this form of pottery is found in many parts of Tibet, and amongst many of the minority peoples of the Ethnic Corridor (Elliott, 2011). In Nangqen

County in Yushu, Qinghai, black pottery has become an important tourist item. A recent issue of the China Daily tells the following story.

> According to an old story, when Princess Wen Cheng passed by Yushu on her way to Tibet in the Tang Dynasty, she taught the pottery manufacturing craft to the local Tibetan people. The pottery-making craft has improved significantly since that time, which has become a way for the Tibetan and Han cultures to integrate…. Qiannang black pottery has been declared a national intangible cultural heritage. Bai Maqunjia, a Tibetan black pottery handicraft man, was also named a national intangible cultural heritage inheritor (China Daily, 2010).

In the Badi region the process of manufacture was different from that of Qiannang in that the black colour resulted from the distinctive colour of the clay. This clay could only be obtained from the high mountains overlooking Badi, and required a climb of several hours to reach the site. Here the clay was gathered and much of the basic work undertaken before it was carried back down to the pottery in the valley. In this volcanic area the clay is rich in iron ore, which on heating produces the distinctive black colour. It also means that the product was surprisingly resistant to thermal shock. The pots can therefore be placed close to the fire to heat the contents and then be removed without cracking as is common with ordinary pots.

The other distinction of this black pottery is that it is not crafted on a wheel, but entirely worked by hand. Using wooden paddles the craftsmen patiently work the clay into thin slabs that are shaped into cylinders or pots. Coils of clay are then pressed into the basic form without disturbing the basic structural integrity, and great care taken in closing the seams. Wooden moulds are often used to give a pattern that is formed with the use of a wooden spatula. Elliot gives a detailed description of Naxi black pottery, which has many similarities in its method of manufacture (Elliott, 2011).

An examination of some of the existing designs shows a variety of uses. First, there are simple flasks used for carrying liquids. These were tied into a leather netting to make them more convenient to carry. Another style of pot is used for drinking the locally made barley alcohol. This is made in the shape of a boot, which is supposed to represent the shoes of the folk hero and protector of the Rgyalrong—A mye Sgo ldung. The alcohol is poured into the vessel and the pot placed at the edge of the fire with the handle away from the flames. The alcohol therefore is warmed and can be drunk through fine straws. On cold evenings the vessel is passed from one person to the next as the family sits around the fire.

Wide variety of vessels made by the apprentices. Here students from SNU are examining the vessels and discussing how they can be improved to make them more attractive to tourists.

The apprentices have made a wide variety of traditional pots, but there is a difference between learning the technology and that of acquiring artistic skill. In the figure above, students are examining the various types of pots that have been made by the apprentices. The artistic skill is what changes the vessel from being a cheaply made local product to a valuable work of art with national or even international recognition. It is this artistic flare that will attract the tourist to buy. In fact, even the local people are not interested in buying a basic pot because they can readily purchase colourful cheap alternatives in the towns. Artistic style is therefore important and this often requires distinctive designs like those of ancient pots.

The major incentive for the younger men to learn this craft was the potential income that could be generated from tourism. However, sales have not been good even though the shop is on a major tourist route. One reason for this is that pots are heavy and another reason is that they lack the artistic flare that is found in some of the Naxi ware. Although the old man was able to pass on the skills for making the pot it was not so easy to pass on the creative ability for making a piece of fine art. Tourists are also looking for items other than traditional forms that have little meaning for them. Napkin rings or Christmas decorations are more likely to find sales with tourists than traditional drinking vessels that can be placed in an open fire. Unless the apprentices are able to explore new opportunities and styles with the clay, this attempt to revive the craft will probably fail.

Silverware

Silverware is common in the area and is brought out for show during festivals. Although, some may actually be of silver metal, many are made from an alloy called "Nickel Silver" or "German Silver". The cheaper alloy was first invented in China with a formulation of 60% copper, 20% nickel and 20% zinc.

Silverware items for men consist of the sheath for a knife, and the distinctive *Gawu*. The word gawu, gauu or ghau (Chinese: 嘎乌) is the transliteration of the Tibetan for "house of the mascot". It is usually a small box with an opening in the shape of a meditating Buddha. Inside is kept a small Buddha statue, a portion of Buddhist scriptures and a relic of the cremation of a Living Buddha of significance to the owner. Among the relics, one of the most important is made from the corpse of the lama in which the blood is mixed with mud to produce a clay tablet. The gawu box is inlaid with agate and turquoise and is carved with a variety of auspicious patterns. The gawu is not primarily a decoration, but an item for spiritual protection—it is in fact a portable shrine. The owner therefore does not like strangers touching their gawu as it is believed that it can cause pollution.

Gawu vary in shape and size, but for men the shape is generally square while for women it is round or oval. Men are very particular about how they wear their gawu, and usually have them hanging in a cloth pouch under their left arm. Women usually wear theirs as a necklace or hanging on a silk rope on their chest as in the figure following. Before the liberation of Tibet there were 8 levels in the Tibetan government. The high-ranking officials rank 4 and above, used to wear a small gawu in their hair-knot as a sign of their official position. The highest officials also placed a wolf tooth inside their gawu as a symbol of their power.

A young woman wearing a popular style of *gawu*.

Although the Rgyalrongwa like gawu, they do not make them. This task is usually done by Han residents in the area. Metalworking is considered to be polluting and so is shunned by the Rgyalrongwa. This work is regarded as a kind of punishment for bad karma coming from previous lives. Both silver-smiths and black-smiths are therefore treated as being of the lowest social class. For example, none of their family or clan members were supposed to serve in the monastery. When Emperor Qianlong conquered Rgyalrong at the end of 18th century AD, he decided to get at least two Han Chinese black-smiths settled to help in every Rgyalrong village.

In contrast, the Qiang people respect the Han metalworkers and will encourage their daughters to marry into these families. The height of their respect is shown in that a white quartz stone representing the metalworker is often enshrined in a corner of their house.

Copper is also a popular metal in the Tibetan area for jewellery and decoration. As it is expensive, in the Rgyalrong area it is mainly used by households for small offering bowls used in the shrine room. It is in the monasteries that larger copper items can be seen. Here craftsmen hammer the soft metal into shape.

Although the gawu was essentially for spiritual protection it always had additional functions such as fashion and a status symbol. The gawu has continued as an item of fashion, but unlike in earlier centuries when it was worn daily it is now only used on special occasions. Gawu are now being sold internationally via the Internet, but the larger Rgyalrong gawu are currently not being sold.

Weaving

Of all the crafts found in Tibet weaving is the one most universally practiced. Every house has its loom and a large proportion of the population, both male and female, claim competence in this work, with the result that the Tibetans have been among the most adequately clothed peoples in the world which was necessary in the harsh climate.

The Tibetan weaver had access to the best possible quality of wool, since sheep living under the hard conditions grow an excellent quality fleece. Even when it feels soft to the touch it retains a resilience that enables it to stand up to the hardest wear. The Tibetans do not make the mistake of depriving the sheep of too much of their natural oil because this is why their cloth is ideal for wearing in a very cold climate. Tibetan rugs are used exclusively for sitting on; never as floor coverings. Mostly they are of small size, oblong or square, being placed upon a low mattress of corresponding size. The only carpets of any considerable size are the long runners used by the rows of monks when engaged in chanting in the main shrines (Pallis, 1967).

Rgyalrong clothing has retained many traditional features even though it has shown some changes as a result of the contact with both Han and Tibetan culture. Many of the common colours and symbols are associated with ancient Tibetan symbols.

Concluding thoughts

During the twentieth century Rgyalrong arts and crafts have exhibited major changes because the mass produced products of China have had a great impact on the local community. As mentioned, many of the traditional arts and crafts have disappeared but a few have now been conserved by encouraging a few old craftsmen to teach younger men. Nevertheless, the traditional crafts such as black pottery have little practical application today as a utilitarian item. Where such skills are preserved it is when the craft is perceived as a form of art that is admired even by outsiders, especially tourists who are willing to pay for the work of local art. Traditional crafts have therefore become seen even by the local people as works of art.

Another issue that emerges is that of whether the product is in fact *authentic* or a fake. Black pottery, for example is also being made by mechanized processes by Han Chinese in the cities, and these could be classed as fakes (inauthentic objects). In this sense the notion of an authentic item lies only in the realm of the museum where some "expert" has designated the item as "authentic". Some experts in ethnic art tend to the view that authentic and fake are actually the two poles of a continuum.

As Cohen has noted most tourists do not demand such total authenticity, but focus on some trait of the cultural product (Cohen, 1988). For example, they like a product that is hand-made by local people using local materials in fairly traditional ways. These traits are considered sufficient for the authentication of the product as a whole.

"Commoditization" is the process where items (and activities) come to be evaluated primarily in terms of their exchange value. The artefact is made for the primary function of trade. "Dealings with strangers … provide contexts for the commoditization of things that are otherwise protected from commoditization" (Appadurai, 1986:15). In this process the product loses its intrinsic meaning and significance for the local people, who in turn lose their enthusiasm for producing the product.

One exception to this trend is when the skill is what can best be described as a hobby. An obvious case of this is the skills of weaving and embroidery. Women especially like to engage in this hobby and grandparents enjoy teaching this skill to their grandchildren. Here the skill is learnt and practiced for personal enjoyment and creativity rather than for utilitarian purposes or financial gain. The products of their work are brought out to be worn and displayed during festive occasions such as celebrations, dances and weddings.

The other exception to the general trend is where the product is used for religious purposes. This is especially seen with the thangka paintings which have important religious functions in temples and monasteries. The skill required in the art and design makes the thangka a work of art in its own right. Although this can be copied and mass produced, such a product is considered to have the spiritual efficacy of a hand painted product produced by a craftsman motivated by devotion. The thangka has retained its place as a piece of fine art, and has become an item of worldwide admiration.

7 Wedding

During the turmoil of the Cultural Revolution many of the traditional rites of passage and calendar rites in China were suppressed because they were considered to be expressions of the old way of life. The following chapters examine how various Rgyalrong rituals have changed and how their distinctive traditional identity may yet be preserved. This chapter will look at marriage.

Tibetan people have had some of the most diverse forms of marriage including polyandry, and these have fascinated western writers. In recent years, Tibetans have increasingly adopted Han Chinese elements into their wedding practices particularly among the young people who have gone to work in the big cities.

The Rgyalrong farmers have continued with patrilocal residence even though an increasing number of young women have moved to the cities for jobs. The following description includes a case study of a wedding in a Rgyalrong family. The wedding discussed took place in the village of Badi, some 40km north of the town of Danba in January 2009. During the last few years a team of staff and students from the Institute of Education, Sichuan Normal University, Chengdu have had frequent contact with this area studying the cultural changes that are occurring. As a result, a cultural centre was established in the village. The people have come to appreciate the way that the team has endeavoured to preserve and record their local traditions. Hence, they were eager to invite the team to a wedding in their village especially as the family sought to follow the traditional marriage ritual. The team not only went to enjoy the festivities, but to make a photographic and video record.

Choosing a bride

The young man in question was the third son of the family living in the town of Badi. He first met the young lady when she was working in the home of an old lady in the same town. The girl came from a village 11km further north up the valley. Although he liked her he was rather shy, and so asked some friends to help him. The relationship quickly developed and the arrangements for the marriage soon began. Although young people are allowed more freedom of choice than in past years, the role of the families is still important as the girl will usually live in the man's household. The family of a man who is looking for a bride therefore have their own criteria as to what makes a suitable wife and member of the household. Their criteria are firstly that she must be respectful of elders and behave in a courteous way to them. Secondly, the girl should be a good cook as cooking for the family will be an important role for her. Finally, an attractive face is not considered very important although it is seen as being an important concern for the young man himself. Today, in the Rgyalrong area there is a shortage of girls as many of them go to work as cooks and dancers in the bigger towns of Kangding and Chengdu. The family are therefore more realistic about the situation and are willing for the young man to find a suitable young lady.

As regards the girl's family they are looking for a man who is honest, respects elders and is a hard worker. In addition, it is considered desirable that he is a non-smoker even though most men do smoke, and that he doesn't drink too much of the locally brewed alcohol. The reputation of the family is however considered to be of particular importance, and the girl's family would make enquires about the boy's family. This was not difficult in the present case as the man's family had a good reputation which was known even 11km away in the girl's village.

Nevertheless, due protocol had to be followed. A group of men from the man's family had to go and see the girl's family about the arrangements for the marriage. During this encounter the man's family were expected to show due deference and humility. The leader of the party would say that they were not a wealthy family nor had a high social status, but would consider it a great honour if the girl was allowed to marry their son. Gifts would then be exchanged.

The date for the wedding was chosen by divination. There are two ways that this can be done. The first is by a diviner who looks at the shape and characteristics of the faces of the young couple and from these he will be able to tell what will be an auspicious day. The second means is by looking at one of various astrological texts, and from the dates of birth of the couple set a suitably auspicious date.

The day prior to the coming of the bride to the man's family home is one of frantic activity for the groom's family. Everyone in the village takes part in cleaning and tidying the village and preparing the wedding banquet. In this case, the family were planning to feed some 600 people at the feast, which included many from the bride's village and other surrounding villages. The dance area is part of the newly built cultural centre and was an ideal location for the meal and entertainment.

In the evening prior to the wedding, the local "speech-maker" (Prins, 2007), as he will be called, came to the home of the groom's family to chant. The speech-maker need not be a monk, but any male who has gained the respect of the community for this role. He began the first of two periods of chanting in the small shrine room at the top of the family house. In this case, the chants came from Bön texts that called the mountain gods to bring prosperity to the young couple. As part of this process, a model elephant was made of red-brown dough to represent the god of wealth (财神, cai shen). As elephants have not been known in this area, this symbol must have originated with Ganesha, the Indian god of wealth, well-known for his elephant head. When I mentioned this to the speech-maker he thought such a relationship was most likely. Around this central figure are placed symbols of "valuable things". The speech-maker said that the elephant represents the household and the valuable things are the dowry and skills of the bride that will come with her into the household. The model and chants are to ask the god that these may continue to stay in the home.

Collecting the Bride

As the morning of the bride's arrival comes, everyone hurries to make final preparations. Tables and stools are laid out in neat rows on the dance area, the streets and paths are swept and relatives of the groom bring gifts of food for the wedding. All gifts were carefully noted down in a logbook to ensure that at any future events the groom's family would reciprocate with an equal or larger gift. It was then time for the bride to be brought.

A party from the groom's family had travelled to the girl's family home. As they approach the home firecrackers are set off and loud music played to signify the event is about to begin. At the bride's home the party is formerly welcomed, and they give gifts of meat, bread and pots of wine. A strangely out-of-place poster of Chairman Mao dominates the main wall of the living room and seems to oversee the proceedings. Further gifts of cloth and clothes are made (Gyu 'brung & Stuard, 2012). The families then begin to make formal conversation, with the groom's family once again taking a humble role. This was especially so as the leader of the groom's party was rather young for this role. He therefore spoke with great respect downplaying the social status of his family which was in fact highly respected in the area. The bride's family accepted the proposal and the gifts, and loud music announced the time of festivities.

Guided by her chaperone, the bride is carried, in the "piggy-back" style, through her village gate by her older brother. If the bride doesn't have any brother, she can pick someone as the brother figure for the wedding. Her wedding party, her close friends and relatives, escort them to the wedding ceremony. The scene is very animated, both by music and by the crying of the bride and her female companions who on the one hand are reluctant to see the bride leaving but on the hand are happy for her.

As the bride is taken away, her villagers line up along the path and sing:

> *Away is our darling girl.*
> *Take good care of her and we*
> *Wish you all the best.*
> *Roses all the way on the wedding road.*

The groom's party reply:

> *Please put your hearts at ease.*
> *We will care for the bride well.*
> *In all things she will have happiness.*

Back and forth, all people from both villages sing songs of their caring and blessings. Friends and families gather to say goodbye to the girl who is dressed in a beautifully embroidered jacket. The family garland the bride with the white scarves (*katak*) so characteristic of Tibetan welcomes and departures. The bride then leaves her family home to the sound firecrackers.

The Arrival of the Bride

Prins in her paper on speechmaking gives a summary of a traditional Rgyalrong wedding in the northern area around the county town of Ma'erkang (Prins, 2007).

> Traditionally the groom's family sends a party of men
> and women (a set number) on horseback to the house
> of the bride. The party takes along one horse, decked
> out in much finery, to collect the bride and convey her

to the bridegroom's paternal house. When the horse is prepared, and the members of the groom's party are in the saddle and ready to go, just before they set out on their important mission, the narrator will be given some money, his fee for services rendered. He then recites the speech about the perfect horse, marking the ritual procession of the bride. After that he leads the horse on its journey back and forth, accompanied by the groom's party.

At the wedding in Badi it was not horses that were sent off to bring the bridal party but two 4x4 vehicles. These were carefully decorated with flowers and white scarves. The drivers were dressed in the traditional Rgyalrong fashion, and they had left with a few men for the bride's home.

In the meantime, buckets of water were being filled and lined up from the door of the groom's house along the road to the edge of the village where the girl would arrive. On the top of each bucket was placed a small branch of leaves which would be used to sprinkle the water. Under the buckets were placed one-yuan notes that the children could take after the bride has arrived. The major participants then hurried to dress in traditional Rgyalrong robes. The groom dressed with the great fox fur hat, thick ruby red robes embroidered with auspicious symbols and a colourful shirt. Not all the men dressed in this way, but only the main participants. All the women however dressed in the black embroidered headgear that is so characteristic of the region.

Throughout all this time the speech-maker was chanting in the shrine room while his young assistant was outside the room making offerings to the mountain gods. This consisted of dipping a flower into a small vessel of wine and shaking the flower causing droplets of wine to be blown in the wind. The assistant also gave a short chant asking the mountain gods to bless the occasion.

The arrival of the bride followed by her maid-of-
honour and other guests from her home village.

Finally, the bride arrived in the car followed by her family in an assortment of other vehicles. The bride was escorted with a number of other unmarried ladies to the first of the buckets of water as shown in the figure above. The bride and single ladies were all dressed in the black and white horizontal striped robes that marked their status as unmarried. When all was organized, the headman of the girl's family led the whole group in a line into the village, sprinkling a little water at each bucket to ensure good fortune. The elders finally reached the family home and were greeted by the elders of the man's family who welcomed them at the door with Tibetan barley wine. Here they were blessed by the speech-maker.

The party was led with due respect into the main sitting room. The headmen of the two families took their places on the seats at the top of the room. The bride's family sat on one side and the groom's family opposite. When the bride arrives at the groom's home the bride and her matron of honour are dressed exactly alike. It has been a tradition to make this a matter of fun with the groom being required to distinguish the bride from the matron of honour, much to everyone's amusement.

The wedding ceremony is centred on the bride's maternal uncle, which seems to reflect the matriarchal tradition of Rgyalrongwa in ancient times. Once the girl has crossed the threshold of the house she is seen as becoming a member of the groom's household. As such she should no longer be shy, but feel and act as one of the groom's family. While this is happening the dowry for the bride is being unloaded from the trailer attached to a tractor that had come from her home village. Items included bedding, boxes of cooking pots and personal effects.

The girl's family were then escorted to the banquet that was now prepared in the dance area of the cultural centre. Here again they were duly welcomed with great respect at the gate of the area. The groom now offers barley wine to all who enter, although some refuse knowing that more wine is soon to come. (See figure below). On entering the area, desks were placed at either side to note the gifts which were mainly cash.

The groom welcoming guests with wine while the bride
and her matron of honour wait modestly behind.

The guests then sit chatting while waiting for the food to be prepared. Soon family and friends rush around with big trays of steaming dishes—ten dishes for each table of eight people. The food included pork dishes, fresh fish and vegetables as well as large quantities of rice. The guests were often red in the face as a result of drinking wine as well as expensive Chinese white wine for the toasts. Entertainment is then provided by various members of the groom's family and friends who sing to the guests. The bride and groom then stand in front of the guests to allow members of both families to come forward and bless the young couple with white or yellow silk scarves (*katak*). Finally it is time for the groom's family to eat while the bride's family rest.

After eating, the groom's family and friends hurry to clear away the food, tidy the dance area and prepare for the dances. The two families and friends then commenced the traditional Rgyalrong circular dances. These were led by the older men and women, but as night fell the young people became more prominent and the dances more modern. It is the guests who celebrate with dancing while the bride sits shyly with her girlfriends. The celebrations continued late into the evening when guests quietly made their ways home.

Discussion

This wedding was a deliberate attempt to retain the traditional Rgyalrong marriage customs, but the people were realistic in understanding that things would not be the same as they were 50 or 100 years ago. This event was not being performed for tourists or visitors, but for their personal enjoyment of their own culture and traditions. Nevertheless there are tensions between retaining elements from the past and adopting the modern. Things have changed. The horse that was mentioned by Prins has now been replaced by the motor car. The traditional speeches once important at such occasions have been reduced to greetings at the arrival of the bride. Loud speakers and microphones provide music for all to enjoy.

The things that have continued were those more closely related to the Bön religion which is still significant in the lives of many of these people. The chants performed by the speech-maker in the shrine room of the house followed the traditional rituals, and the mountain gods were invited to come and bless the couple and the occasion. The buckets of water lined up along the path to the groom's home were still seen as important expressions of blessing, and the children enjoyed collecting the one-yuan notes.

In addition to the religious elements, the dances, dress and feasting were also retained. These particular aspects of Rgyalrong culture give a visible expression of their distinctive way of life. Today, central government is seeking to promote intangible heritage, and songs and dances are an obvious cultural expression. Even here, modern Han Chinese music played an important role in the entertainment especially with the young people later in the evening.

One aspect that shows the changes taking place in the community was the fact that prior to the marriage celebration the couple had already obtained the legal certificate of marriage. The festival was a celebration of the girl coming to live with the man's family and becoming part of the patrilocal family. The substantial meal of the social gathering had as much to do with the social standing of the families concerned as with their desire to retain traditions.

In the early morning of the following day, as the team were taking leave of the family, it was the young bride who was busy cooking breakfast for the guests. She was now a member of her husband's family and would make her contribution to the household. Soon however, the young couple left the family home to go back to work in the town.

Usually within a year or so, a child is expected of the union, which actually happened with this couple. Today among the Han people a good proportion of women go to hospital to deliver the baby by caesarean. This is done so that the family can time the birth of the child for their general convenience. Among the Rgyalrongwa however, women still prefer to give birth in the natural way which usually takes place at the woman's family home. The young wife would go to her family home a little before the birth is due so she can receive the support of her mother. She will then stay at her family home for a period of one month after which her husband will come to take her back to his father's house. This child is part of his family following the patrilocal pattern, and the wife will be assisted in looking after the child by her happy mother-in-law. The one-child policy does not apply to the Rgyalrong who are classified as belonging to the Tibetan *minzu*. Thus, most Rgyalrong families will have three or four children. The cycle of life continues.

8 Death - Mortuary Rites

Wave to you silently,
Bid farewell to our fate reincarnation.
Please take away all glories of my life.
Walk by the home once upon a time gently.
God-vultures gathered.
Please open my sunny heavenly way.
So peaceful, so serene, What a wonderful and magical
time
Death is disappearing and the life is flying
Away on the wings.

Song: sky burial / sky dream
Songwriters, Er Mao & Lao zai.

This translation of a popular Tibetan song draws out some of the concepts of sky burial (Chinese: *tianzang*), which still remains an optional mortuary rite among the people of Rgyalrong. This form of mortuary rite often causes reactions of horror from visitors to Tibet, but for many Tibetans themselves it is still regarded as the most excellent way for liberation from the body.

In the 1960s, the government of the People's Republic of China prohibited the practice of sky-burial as being barbaric. In Han Chinese society, burying the corpse following the correct rituals has long been considered as the most appropriate practice. Failure to do this was considered to bring bad fortune upon the family. However, in the

1980s the practice of sky burial was once again allowed, but with some restrictions. Non-Tibetans were not permitted to observe it, and direct photography was considered unethical and offensive and so was forbidden. It was filmed, with permission from the family, for Frederique Darragon's documentary *Secret Towers of the Himalayas* where great care was taken not to show the corpse itself (F. Darragon, 2008).

As mortuary rites compose one of the most important group of Tibetan ritual performances there are many different ritual texts. These have been studied by various scholars (Brauen, 1982; Ramble, 1982; Skorupski, 1982). Many of the funeral studies have also focused upon complex religious rituals and the set texts of one or other of the schools of Tibetan Buddhism. One common assumption made about Tibetan society is that there is a similarity in customs across an enormous area of Central Asia, but there are many local variations especially at the margins of the historical Tibetan area of influence. This has been studied in terms of the "Great" (philosophical) and "Little" (popular) traditions, which helpfully distinguish local aspects of rituals.

The Tibetan Buddhist tradition absorbed many pre-Buddhist (Bön) ideas and practices making it difficult to obtain an accurate idea of what existed prior to the advent of Buddhism. We do know that shamanistic tradition was deeply concerned with the spirits of the dead, and skilled ritual specialists carried out elaborate funeral rites. Bön priests formulated 360 ways of dying, four ways of preparing graves, and 81 ways of taming evil spirits (Bansal, 1994). Sky-burial was one means of disposing of the corpse at that time and seems to reflect the challenges of the environment. The earth was too hard to dig graves, and fuel for cremation was too scarce and costly so that it was an option only for wealthy or illustrious people such as renowned lamas.

Even though ancient Buddhism rejected the notion of an enduring soul, Samten Karmay argues that "Buddhism was never able to suppress the concept of soul in Tibet" (D. S. Lopez, 1996). The *la (bla)*, translated as "spirit", "life-force", or "life-essence" should not be confused with the self, but nonetheless it is highly individuated. In Tibet, a person is believed to have an individual *la* that can wander away and be lost and thus cause psychological disorientation or psychosis. There are specific rituals that can be performed to draw the *la* back to the body (Tsomo, 2001).

This chapter focuses on the life and death of ordinary people living in the Rgyalrong valley in the area of Danba. In this area there are five possible funerary practices: sky burial, water burial, burial in the earth, cremation and stupa burial. We shall examine the contemporary mortuary rites among the people of the Dadu valley, and the forces of change that are occurring. As with mortuary rites in most societies they reveal much about the underlying cosmology of the people. Dealing with death is the last rite of passage.

Five Mortuary Rites

Burial in the earth has been a common practice among the Han Chinese as with many societies. Today, among the Rgyalrongwa it is also a common custom, but it is not one that is regarded as being the most honourable. The local carpenter would construct a coffin made of thick timber similar to that used by Han Chinese, and the burial location is usually some quiet area on the hills above the village. The grave is marked by a white-washed stone, and Tibetan prayer flags are hung around the burial ground. These once brightly coloured flags gradually lose their colours in the rain and wind, becoming limp and grey. The reason why burial is not highly regarded among the Rgyalrongwa will become evident later after sky-burial is discussed in more detail. It is sufficient here to state that earth burial requires a long time before the corpse decomposes.

Water burial is the second means of disposal of the body. In the valleys of southern Tibet or along the Yellow River where there are only a few vultures, water burial is a more common practice than on the grasslands. Rinchen and Kevin (Rinchen rdo rje & Kevin, 2009) have described the simple practice of water burial that is used among the Amdo Tibetans. The corpse is wrapped in either a blanket or white cloth and is carried on a stretcher by the male members of the family to the banks of the Yellow River. The rest of the funeral procession follows them. Ropes are tied around the waists of two men which are held firm by other members of the village. They wade into the river with the corpse until the water reaches their necks, and then the corpse is allowed to drift away with the current.

As it takes many days before the corpse is eaten by the fish, water burial like earth burial is not highly regarded. In fact, water funerals are usually given to the lowest class of people such as beggars, widows, widowers, orphans and the childless. It is used for those who have committed suicide and so are regarded as being spiritually polluted. It is also commonly used in the Rgyalrong region for babies. The body may simply be placed as a whole in the river, or where the water is not sufficiently deep, cut into portions. In the areas where water burial is practiced the local people are careful not eat the fish.

Cremation is a third method for the disposal of a corpse, and is usually permitted only for lamas and some of those of noble birth. As already noted this practice is expensive because of the general shortage of trees especially on the grasslands. A mason is invited to the designated spot to build a stupa-like cremation oven in which the corpse is placed and the fire lit. Michael Vinding in his study of the Thakalis of Nepal in the 1970s showed that cremation was the most common method of disposing of the body (Vinding, 1982). Here the corpse was placed in a cremation kiln either in the standing or seated position. In the Rgyalrong area cremation is uncommon. When the rite is performed monks will chant, and a lama will make appropriate offerings. After the cremation the ashes are taken to a high mountain and thrown into the wind to be blown away or they are thrown into a river to be washed to the sea.

A fourth form is "stupa burial" (*shit a shi*), which is only for those of highest religious status because their spirit is believed to have already become dissociated from bodily things. In this case the body undergoes antiseptic treatment by washing with special herbs for three of four days, and is then put in the sun until it is thoroughly dried. This process is repeated, and finally the corpse is wrapped in white cloth and placed in a casket of gold or silver. Generally, golden caskets are for Dalai Lamas and Panchen Lamas, and silver for high ranking "Living Buddhas" (*tulku*) at important monasteries. These mummified bodies soon became the focus of worship for lay people, and the monastery became a centre for pilgrimage. A lesser form is when the ashes of the person are placed in a stupa (*hui ta shi*).

Although Tibetans realize that to outsiders sky burial is considered disrespectful as a funeral rite, to the Tibetans themselves it is regarded as a very acceptable means for disposing of the body. Martin in his study of the cultural ecology of the Himalayan Plateau comes to the following conclusions as to why sky burial became a common practice.

> In summary, it may be argued that land suitable for burial was scarce for a combination of reasons: 1) Agricultural land was too limited. 2) Most other land was rocky. 3) All land was frozen for the greater part of the year. Fuel suitable for cremation was likewise in low supply because: 1) The most available tree species did not make good firewood. 2) In the few places where good firewood could be found, it was in demand for building purposes. 3) Transportation of lumber was difficult and expensive. 4) Deforestation. (Martin, 2013, 364).

For the people of the valleys however, it is not easy for sky burial to be practiced as it requires the conveyance of the corpse to some high point, which may take two or more days. Before discussing the procedure of sky-burial, it is necessary to discuss how the appropriate mortuary rite is chosen.

When a person dies, it is said that the body should remain at the home for at least three days. This is because people believe that the soul (*li*) may still be alive even if the body is not breathing. During these days the family will invite monks to chant sutras to open the way to the afterlife. Monks will cut out a piece of the scalp of the deceased's head to help the soul leave the body and go directly to the heavenly realm. They will then wash the deceased with holy water and divine the date and the way of the funeral.

As has already been mentioned, some forms of mortuary rite are restricted to those who have attained high spiritual status. It is only high lamas who can receive stupa burial and lesser lamas or noblemen cremation. If the person has been cut to death, shot, died of poison or a contagious disease, sky burial is not permitted. For those whose death is considered "bad", water burial is practiced.

For the elderly, earth burial is now the normal practice, but most of the older people still speak in wistful terms of the hope of sky-burial. This is considered the best mortuary rite for a layperson. In order to fulfil this desire their family may arrange to transport the corpse from the valleys onto the grasslands, and then to the sacred areas for sky-burial. The practice of sky burial varies from place to place, but the following description is typical.

Practice of the sky burial

In the Rgyalrong language, sky burial is called *bya.'bod.ka.lad* (Chinese: 天葬, Pinyin: tianzang, literally "Sky-burial"). There are two kinds of person who work as professional sky burial masters: a distinctive class of monks, and those who were once monks and have renounced their vows and are now lay people. The position of sky-burial master is assigned by the temple, and the person will learn the task from an older master. Sometimes the master will pass the job on to his son. Masters can make a lot of money for their services, but the local people consider them polluted and filled with viruses and ghosts. They usually have few friends and are only able to marry girls from the families of another sky-burial master.

The actual rituals vary from region to region, but there is a common overall practice. If the person is considered suitable for sky-burial, the master will clean the body and tie it in a foetal position with hands meeting on the chest and seated with folded legs. Traditionally, on the funeral day, the master arrives at four in the morning, and draws two white lines of flour outside the house of the dead about one metre apart. He carries the body on his back and walks in-between the lines. This means that the ghost will not return to disturb the living. When the sun appears on the body it is carried to the funeral ground, which is usually a rock in some isolated spot on the hillside near the temple. According to some books, it is said that there are two special rocks for this purpose. One is *Sela* rock in Tibet and the other is *Kangba Xiaduka* rock in Luhuo luozong area in Ganze autonomous prefecture in the west of Sichuan province. They are said to have flown magically from India. However, the sky burial occurs in many parts of the grasslands, and so in practice there are numerous sites.

The journey often involves a circumambulation around a sacred mountain, a sacred lake or a sacred place such as a monastery with which the person was associated. The circumambulation around the mountain or lake has to be accomplished three times in a clockwise direction, and often involves a considerable journey of many miles and will take several days. One way that this was accomplished was that the corpse was wrapped in a cloth and then seated in a car tyre, so that the body was wedged in place. The tyre with the body was then carried on a man's back with the head facing backwards.

From about 2010 a new development occurred in that the whole procedure became commercialised. It is now possible to have the body taken around the mountain or lake on a motorcycle. However, because the act has been mechanized it does not involve as much physical effort, and for this reason a leading Geshe (teacher) has decided that it will require three times as many circumambulations. That is nine times! The body is wrapped in something like a body-bag, and unceremoniously slung over the back of the motorcycle. As the rider often has to stop overnight, the body is left outside the camp. As several bodies are disposed of at the same time, the motorcycle riders try to arrive at the burial site at the same time to make a bigger impression.

The burial-master will put aromatic herbs on a fire to cause it to smoke which acts as a signal to the vultures. They recognize the sign, and fly toward the area from all directions until scores, or even hundreds of vultures alight on the surrounding hills. Then the monks begin to chant sutras to ghosts in order to make the soul of the deceased drift to the world of the dead through the top of the head. The master then dissects the corpse. There are variations in how this is done, but the aim is to make the corpse easier for the vultures to eat. In one region the corpse is strung up on a rock or wooden frame, and cut from shoulder to shoulder, and down the two sides. The skin with the attached flesh is then wrenched away from the skeletal frame, which then can collapse onto the ground. In other cases the cut on a man commences with the eye and goes down the face and body. For a woman the cut often begins around the breasts and then down the body. The dismembered body is then laid front downward ready for the vultures.

Strangely, the vultures tend to line up in rows to eat the body and only a limited number go to the first body. When the second body is ready a similar number will go to that body, and so on. It only takes ten minutes, or so, for the body to be consumed with each vulture eating as much as seven or eight kilos. When the flesh has all been eaten, the master will break and powder the bones. He will then mix this with *tsampa* (Tibetan barley flour) and toss the flour balls to the vultures. When the vultures have left, the master puts away his knives and utensils, scrubs the blood off his hands with tsampa and drinks butter tea. If the corpse has not been entirely eaten, it will be cremated.

It is said that even if only the smell of blood is left on the ground, the spirit of the deceased cannot rise to the heavenly realm. If the vultures completely eat the body this indicates that the deceased did not live a sinful life, so the soul is able to ascend to heaven. If the body is not entirely eaten it means the deceased was guilty of some sin, or even that the person was evil during his or her lifetime. This makes it difficult for the soul to ascend to heaven. The family members then have to invite some monks to continue chanting for his or her soul. Sky burial is therefore carried out at a time when the master knows the vultures have not previously eaten. If the bodies of both men and women need to be taken for sky burial at the same time, the male corpse is dealt with first, and then that of the woman. This, it is said, is not because a man has special privileges, but that the flesh of a woman is easier for the vultures to swallow than that of a man.

In Tibetan thinking, vultures are god-birds and the embodiment of *Dakini*—a Tantric deity described as a female embodiment of enlightened energy. In the Tibetan language, *dakini* is rendered *khandroma*, which means "she who traverses the sky" or "she who moves in space". Sometimes the term is translated poetically as "sky dancer" or "sky walker". Often a solitary white-breasted eagle (probably a Steppe Eagle, *Aquila nipalensis*) is seen circling high above, and this bird is known as "mercy mother walking the skies".

After the sky burial, the monks were also invited to chant inside the deceased's home for 49 days following the death. Relatively affluent families would also dedicate some money to the nearby temple and request them to continue chanting for the deceased. Rinchen and Kevin (Rinchen rdo rje & Kevin, 2009) describe the feast provided in an Amdo funeral. In this case after the full 49 days, the family asked more monks to chant, and invited relatives to come to their house to help chant for the deceased. One year later and three years later, the family will light the butter lamps to mourn and pray for the deceased.

The reason for the 49 days of chanting is that Buddhism teaches that after death, and before the rebirth, there is a period of 49 days when the soul roams in *Nardo*—the state between life and death. If the person has lived a very good life they will be reborn on the seventh day. If not, they may be reborn on the 14th, 21st, 28th, 35th, 42nd or 49th days. If the deceased is not reborn upon the 49th day, they will not be reborn as a human, but as an insect in the vegetables, fruits or stones. During the forty-nine days the deceased's family members would therefore keep burning money and food as an offering for the deceased. They request the monks to continue chanting to help the dead to be reborn as soon as possible and have a good life in the next reincarnation. On the 49th day villagers are convinced that the deceased has been reborn, so fasting takes place again.

It is an ancient custom that the sky burial master can take away all the deceased's things in his bed. This is associated with a story about a rich man who did not have children, but a lot of gold. He did not like his servant and did not want to give his gold to anyone else, so he put all the gold ingots on his person. When the funeral master came to carry the body he found it very heavy and discovered the gold. As it was his right to have everything lying on the bed he carried away the gold ingots with the body.

The family of the deceased are not allowed to attend the ceremony, and many do not want to attend for obvious reasons. The family does however want to be assured that the body has been correctly disposed of, so they would ask three witnesses to attend the event. These witnesses are chosen so that they do not know each other, but are willing to attend the ceremony. Each will separately be given a small piece of bone from the right shoulder, which they have to take back to the family. The bone in the shoulder is chosen because it does not have any marrow. The spiritual essence of the person is considered as residing in the body fluid, and so as this is lacking in this bone it contains none of the essence of the person. Once the family have the three pieces of bone they will fit them together, to ensure that they are all from the same body.

Mythical origins of the sky burial

A common story among the Rgyalrongwa tells of the origin of sky burial.

> Long, long ago, there was a king in Nepal, who had two sons. The youngest prince judged other people with charity and kindness. One day, when the king, his wife, two sons and various ministers went out in the woods they saw a tigress who had just given birth to six tigers.

She was extremely hungry at this time and exhausted from the birth. The younger prince said "This tigress is about to die of hunger and is likely to eat her babies." The younger prince asked "What does a tigress eat." The king replied, "Only slaughtered meat with blood will satisfy it." Then, the younger prince thought "I am going to donate my body to save the tigress".

When the royal family had moved away from the animal, the prince said he had something to do and let them walk on. He ran back to the tigress and offered himself to the animal. However, the mouth of the tigress was too dry, so it could not eat. The younger prince then picked up a spiny stick and stabbed himself to get blood. The tigress licked his blood and then was able to eat the prince. The king waited for the younger prince for a long time and then realized what the prince had said. They ran back to the tigress and found that the tigress had eaten the younger prince's body. The king and queen fainted with grief.

The younger prince is said to have been reborn into the heavenly realms. There he saw that his parents were inconsolable at his death, and he had pity on them. He therefore came to them to comfort them and said "Because I saved the tigress I have been reborn in *tusita* realm. You should know all life must end. Evil people must fall into hell; merciful people will be reborn into the *tusita deva*-world. Life and death are both very natural and normal. Why not be awakened and work hard to do good?" The king and queen buried his bones within a temple above the site of the event.

This is an adaption of one of the well-known *Jataka* stories of the previous incarnations of Shakyamuni Buddha that were originally written in the ancient Indian language of Pali. In the Tibetan tradition the story has been reinterpreted to imply that sky burial follows the example of the Buddha who offered his body to feed animals. In the Tibetan language the practice is called "*du chui jie wa*", which means "off (corpse) to the burial field". It is also known as "*qia duo*" meaning "feeding the vulture" or "bird burial". There is no specific record of when sky burial first began in Tibet, but it seems to be an ancient custom unique to the high altitudes of the Central Asian plateau. Vajrayana Buddhism provided a religious rational for this old practice as it was contextualized to Tibetan culture.

Death is seen as the beginning of new life through reincarnation, but the continuing physical presence of the body hinders an early rebirth of the soul. As the body is seen merely as the carrier of the soul, once this role is finished the body no longer has any value. Sky burial therefore provides purpose for the body, because, just as with the *Jataka* story, it is donated to reduce the hunger pains of the vultures. The vultures eat dead bodies and then fly high into the sky such that the soul ascends to the heavenly realms. Sky burial is considered by the Tibetans to be the most thorough and rapid mortuary practice.

The corpse is also an offering presented to the gods for a redemption of the sins of the deceased. Everyone will one day die, so the things we have now cannot be possessed forever. It is said that the attitude of generosity shown by the giving of the deceased's body will arouse feelings of compassion in the people who come to the sky ground. From these feelings they will begin to repent and live more honourable lives.

Contemporary understandings of sky burial

As was mentioned earlier, with the establishment of New China the practice was banned, but the practice was again permitted in the 1980s. There were two practical reasons for this change of policy. First, since the ritual was performed in isolated places, it was difficult to police. Second, in much of Tibet the ground is too hard and rocky to dig a grave, and with fuel and timber scarce, a sky burial is often more practical than cremation.

A new perspective on sky burial has recently emerged among younger people. They consider it to be both environmentally friendly and bringing harmony between humans and animals. Firstly, compared with the burial in the earth, the sky burial does not leave the dead body to decay in a grave. There is no grave that needs to be repaired, it is less polluting to the earth, and it conserves land for other uses. Secondly, compared with water burial, sky burial is less polluting and wasteful, and has no adverse effects on the fish and animals living in the water. Compared with cremation, sky burial does not pollute the air. Associated with this is the account told by the local people that a vulture knows the date when it will die. Seven days before its death the vulture flies higher and higher in the sky until it slowly disappears in the atmosphere, not leaving any part of its body.

The mortuary ritual of "sky burial" is consequently still highly regarded by the Rgyalrong people. The deeply held religious ideas of the people provides a meaningful explanation such that sky burial is thought of as the most pure, and the most sacred burial custom. It is therefore not surprising that this practice has continued during all the changes of the last hundred years.

9 Zalajusong: The dance of the fighting gods

High in the hills to the East of the Rgyalrong valley are two villages Da Ping and Xiao Ping (Literally 'Great Ping' and 'Small Ping'). Together they are known as Erjiping and have a population of about 500 persons. Because of their relative isolation these villages have been subject to less change in the twentieth century than many of the villages along the river valley. This chapter attempts not only to document and record a distinctive dance of the village, but also to understand the historical and social meaning. For political reasons the dance stopped in 1954, but in 1983 the local area officials asked them to recommence the dance as a possible tourist attraction. At that time the village elders asked 16 people to be volunteers to re-establish this dance and it is from this group that the current dance team finally emerged. It has been difficult to continue the dance as the equipment and clothes are expensive. Even though some items like the helmet, shoes and shield can be made in the village, other items have to be bought from outside.

Questions about the history and symbolism of the dance often raised the reply that there was once a book that contained all the information, but this was lost during the time of the Cultural Revolution. In 2007, the main informant was the oldest man of the village who was then 85 years of age. He died in 2011. The old people only had limited knowledge of the meaning of the dance, and it is out of these memories that the dance has once again been revived.

Before discussing the possible history and symbolism of the dance, I want to describe the dance that I first witnessed on 27th February 2007 with a team from Sichuan Normal University who were seeking to document the dance. On later occasions, the team and I again witnessed the performance.

Description of the Dance

Prior to the dance a monk would chant continuously for 24 hours. We were informed that in earlier times it was not a monk who chanted, but a shaman. This chanting is believed to cause the evil forces of the region to gather in the dance area where they can be dealt with. There are many words in Tibetan for spiritual powers. Two words are of particular importance in this context - *doerma* and *dongi*. *Doerma* are evil spirits and although they cannot be destroyed, they can be brought under control and expelled from the village so that they no longer pose a danger. *Dongi* are best understood as ghosts—the spiritual essence of deceased people who afflict misfortune upon the living. Unlike the *doerma,* the *dongi* can be destroyed which is the purpose of the ritual.

The main dance commenced in the afternoon of the tenth day of the first month of the Chinese lunar calendar. People gather early to find suitable seats around the rectangular dance area, which has long been the main communal area of the village. In the centre was erected a pole reaching 20 metres into the air. This was adorned with prayer flags and topped with the national flag of the People's Republic of China. Around this flagpole were arranged tables on which alcohol, fruit and other items were placed. The event was introduced with lots of notices and expressions of gratitude that reverberated through the village amplified by the loudspeaker system.

The 13 dancers finally emerged from a neighbouring house and waited for the introductions to end before entering the dance area. They were led into the ground by a dancing snow lion which was animated by two dancers. The dancers played with some of the little boys in the watching audience who were intrigued at the sight. Following them were the two monks currently resident in the area, and then the elders of the village. The dancers followed the procession and everyone circled the ground. The customary white silk scarves were then given by the monks as a token of recognition to the people who had arranged this particular dance. The people then seated themselves and allowed the 13 dancers to take up their positions.

The dancers arranged themselves in a wide circle around the central pole when the military nature of their dress and stance was obvious. The dancers wore coloured helmets with long bird feathers. On their backs they carried shields decorated with various designs, and in their hands they carried a bow, but no arrows. Strapped to the waist of each dancer was a sword. Then two musicians with drum and cymbals started to play. The dance was vigorous and demanded strength and stamina as one would expect from soldiers. The sweeping movements often ended in a kneeling position in which the dancers drew their bows as if shooting an arrow. As the dancers did not have any arrows their swords were used in their place. When dancing with their swords, the soldiers also used long sweeping movements demonstrating their dexterity and power.

Dance of the Thirteen Fighting Gods: dancer with bow and sword.

The final stage of the dance was perhaps the most symbolic. The dancers gradually moved in a spiral pattern closer to the centre of the circle, and when within a couple of metres of the post they thrust their swords into the ground. The dancers then backed away to the outer part of the dance area leaving 13 swords in a circle stuck into the ground around the central post. The dancers then moved back to their swords, but they did not simply pick up their swords, but jumped back with a shout as if they were hesitant to again take up their swords. They then moved forward a second time and this time they withdrew their swords.

Dancers thrusting their swords into the ground.

Thanks were then given by the master of ceremonies to the team for filming the dance, and white scarves were once again given before the second and shorter section of the dance began. In this dance the old man seated at the edge of the circle sang with a clear voice. The dancers responded while moving around in a less vigorous circular dance. They were joined by three other singers and dancers to make a total of 16 in the dance. After some 10 minutes the dance came to an end and the warriors walked from the dance area. The performance ended with photographs being taken of those who had arranged the event and the monks seated in the place of honour.

This was a very different style of dance than those found in other parts of the Dadu River valley. The dress was distinctive as was the choreography which demonstrated military strength and agility.

Organization and changes to the dance

Various changes had been made to the dance in recent years, and these show some of the issues that the people had struggled with concerning the dance and even whether it should be continued. For this poor village, a main issue was the finance of the dance. Initially the cost had been paid for by the people who participated in the dance with contributions from their families. However, this could mean that some families would make no contribution for several years. In 2006 it was decided that the organization of the dance and payment should be made according to the twelve animal years. As 2007 was the year of the pig, it was for those born in the years of the pig to make the arrangements. It was these people who were especially recognized by the monks with the offering of scarves in the festival.

Because of the cost and work involved in making the costumes some changes have been made. One notable feature concerned the headgear. Previously these were conical in shape and made from woven sticks, but this year they were simply made of card and brightly decorated although retaining the same shape.

According to the old man who was our main informant, the men who used to take part in the dance were those who were 49 years of age. He said that some people thought that the dance was all that remained of a more complex series of rituals that were performed for men in their 49th year. The most likely explanation for this age is that it was the age that men retired from the army of the Rgyalrong king. It was therefore the age that they changed roles from being soldiers to being elders of the village. This would be consistent with the martial theme of the dance and could explain some of the symbolism.

In 2007 the dance team consisted of younger men. Three were aged 41, two were 40, nine were between 20–29 and two were still in their teens. Now if a man wants to quit the team he must choose a substitute and teach him all he has learned. Such a person needs to be strong and a good dancer.

To prepare for the dance in 2007, the community was given a donation from the Ford Foundation to pay for new costumes and equipment. The people were clearly pleased with this donation, but were still uncertain about the source of future funding. There was some disagreement in the community concerning the continuation of the dance. Generally the older generation (over 35) wanted to continue the dance, while younger people were uncertain about its value and usefulness. It was however notable that the children were excited to have the dance, which brought a welcome holiday atmosphere to the daily life in this small village.

Symbolism of the Dance

As mentioned earlier, the people said the meaning and symbolism of the dance had been written in an ancient book that was now lost. Elements of the symbolism could therefore only be gathered from the memories of the old men. The following is a collection of these thoughts.

The military element of the dance distinguished it from other dances in the Rgyalrong valley. Mongol forces had frequently invaded the valley from the north and the people of this region had distinguished themselves as great fighters. Later during the Jiarong Wars they were frequently in conflict as the region erupted in turmoil with the socio-political struggle between the Rgyalrong and Bön religion on one side, and the Manchus and dGelugpa on the other. According to Karmay, in 1776, after six years of conflict, the Manchus finally triumphed when they defeated the heartland of Rgyalrong culture which was around the modern city of Jinchuan just a few miles north of Erjiping (Karmay, 2005, 5-8). The Bön monastery of the Rab brtan royal house was destroyed and a dGelugpa monastery built on the site with authority over the other dGelugpa establishments in Rgyalrong. Emperor Qianlong was anxious to spread dGelugpa tradition in the region in order to bring Rgyalrong firmly under imperial control

Today, the border between the conquered area in the north of the valley and the south is still evident. In the north the population has more mixed ethnic origins and the houses built more in the style of the Han Chinese whereas in the south, the housing and population is that of the traditional Rgyalrong. Erjiping lies on the hill at the northernmost part of the traditional Rgyalrong kingdoms. The monastery now overlooking the village is dGelugpa (Yellow-hat) and most people consider themselves dGelugpa, and the Bön and Red-hat traditions to be superstitions. Nevertheless in the village, internal conflicts continue between the Red-hat and Yellow-hat traditions. The Red-hat monastery further up the main valley continues to send books and DVDs to the village to encourage them in this tradition.

The costume used in the dance was similar to that used by soldiers in the Qing dynasty of the eighteenth and nineteenth century. Old photographs from the early 1900s show Chinese soldiers of an unidentified militia unit in a similar style of dress ("Qing Imperial Polearms," accessed 27 March 2014.). This shows how the Manchu influence was strong even after the Second Jairong War, and there was considerable mixing of styles. Documents show that Emperor Qianlong was so impressed by the dance that he wanted it performed every year in Beijing.

A second element is that many people consider that the 13 warriors represented 13 divinities who entered the sacred space to defeat the forces of evil that have been gathered. Thirteen is considered to be a lucky number in Tibetan cosmology because heaven is believed to be composed of 13 layers, and the thirteenth heaven is the Pure Land described by Tsongkhapa, founder of the Yellow-hat tradition. The

13 dancers thus represent traditional gods who had come to assist the community in its fight against evil.

Evidence for this comes from a large thangka depicting Murdo the god of the sacred peak Mt Murdo near the town of Danba. The representation on the thangka is very similar to Dorje Shugden, who has been the centre of debate with regards to the current Dalai Lama (Batchelor, 1998). Dorje Shugden is one of a pantheon of 'protector deities' known as *Chos skyong* (Skt. *Dharmapala*) or 'Dharma-protectors'. These deities are said to have vowed to serve and protect the Buddha's teaching and its practitioners. The 13 local gods could be considered as being of this class of Dharma-protectors

Contemporary relevance of an ancient dance

As mentioned earlier, in 2007 there was controversy in the community as to the contemporary relevance of the dance. Critics saw it as costly and time consuming although they did acknowledge its potential as a tourist attraction. In fact just two days prior to the dance I observed, they had performed to a group of 17 people from Taiwan who had been invited by a monk who had visited Taiwan. This was the first time that they had performed the dance for tourists. People were however uncertain about the financial rewards of the dance even though all had heard stories of the financial gains made by other minority communities from tourism. Erjiping however is only accessible by a very narrow road that zigzags up the steep hillside at the top of which is a level area of land on which the village is sited. The dance would be the only particular item of interest for tourists apart from the beautiful scenery but since 2007, few tourists have made the steep climb. The fact that the dance has continued despite the lack of tourists therefore shows that there are other reasons why the people wish to preserve the performance.

It was not until about the year 2000 that their village was caught up in the changes that have been taking part in other areas of China.

It was at this time that many of the children went out of the village for their schooling. Parents have recently become keen for their children to find jobs with the local government, which requires at least 9 years of schooling. In the minds of the parents therefore schooling has come to be associated with finding government jobs, and they see little other value for schooling as young people can always go to the towns to find jobs as dancers and singers or working on building sites in the Amdo region. The fact that the younger generation is going out of the village means that they are wanting to embrace the comforts of a modern lifestyle. The older generation however are eager to hold on to their customs which they see as having continuing value.

Many of the older people are also beginning to learn Tibetan writing, which they are studying during summer and winter periods when farm work is less busy. This is encouraged by the dGelugpa monks for whom the Tibetan script is an important part of their literal tradition. Although the people consider Tibetan to be an important part of their cultural heritage, the local spoken language is part of the Rgyalrong language cluster. The older people therefore appear to be adopting more of Tibetan culture in order to retain what they imagine to be their traditional culture. It seems therefore that since about 2000 the religious aspect of the culture has become more Tibetan while the economic aspect has become more Han.

Returning to the subject of the dance itself, at the request of their parents many of the young people do come home for the dance that is held on 10th and 11th day after Chinese Spring Festival. The first few days of the Chinese Spring Festival are a busy and lucrative time for the young people who are dancers and singers, and they come home only for the end part of the two-week holiday. Dancing for them has become a way of making money, and the religious significance of this dance for them is of little or no importance. Thus, although they take part in the dance for them the dance has become secularized.

The continuation of the dance results from the fact that the local people want to retain something of their distinctive social identity in a period of rapid social change. The dance is one of the few expressions that remain of their history and culture. It shows they are the inheritors of a distinct social and political community that once existed in the Rgyalrong valley although they now consider themselves to be part of the wider Tibetan community.

10 A Rgyalrong New Year Festival

The Rgyalrong people have many festivals that are distinct from those practiced in Lhasa far to the west. One example of a calendar festival is seen in the New Year festival of the people of the village of Qiong Shan, a small village high above the town of Badi which is located on the banks of the Dadu River. What is particularly interesting is that public celebration of this festival ended in 1952 when the local *tusi* (king) was deposed. Although some elements of the ritual have been continued by some families in the confines of their own homes, by 2006 only four old men remained who could remember the communal aspect of the festival. (Prins, 2006). This chapter will commence with an account of how the villagers sought to reconstruct their particular New Year festival in 2006, and how the festival has changed during the following few years.

It is first necessary to emphasise that the Rgyalrong New Year does not occur at the same time as the Tibetan New Year (*Losar*). The Tibetan New Year commences on the first day of the first lunar month, which is the day of the new moon. Its name derives from *lo* meaning "new" and *sar* meaning "year". It predates the coming of Buddhism, being associated with the Bön religion, and varies in how it is celebrated in different parts of the Tibetan world. In Lhasa, in preparation for the *Losar* celebration households make *kasai* (fried twisted dough sticks) in various forms, and *luoguo* (a kind of food made of butter in the shape of a sheep's head), signifying thriving domestic animals and abundant life. There is also a "Festival of Banishing Evil Spirits" when people will wave burning torches and shout to rid their houses of evil spirits. During the first two days of the festival people visit their neighbours, exchange *Tashidelek* blessings, and enjoy eating together. Dried or fresh fruits, butter and brick tea are offered to the Buddhas, and the old prayer flags are replaced with new ones. In 2007 *Losar* began on February 18th six weeks after the Rgyalrong festival we are about to describe.

Key themes

As with many festivals several important themes come together in the symbolism of the ritual. Before describing the ritual it is necessary to explain some of these themes.

First, as pointed out already, the festival did not take place at *Losar*, but two, or sometimes six weeks earlier on the 12th-15th days of the month of the Tiger. This date is set by when the full Moon crosses over the star system known as Pleiades (or M45). As the Pleiades are 4 degrees north of the ecliptic, it can be occulted only when the Moon's orbit is in Pisces-to-Sagittarius part of the ecliptic. The situation repeats every 18.6 years, and during a period of some 6 or 7 years there may be several occultations. This happened 13 times in 2006 and will continue to a lesser degree until 2010. In Eastern Asia it occurred on 31st December 2006 with an 88% waxing of the Moon (Rao, 2005). The six dots representing the star system (a line of 4 dots and a parallel line of 2) are found in various aspects of the festival.

A second element is the story of the local hero *Amigeerdong* who fought a ghost that according to legend, used to eat one person a day from the village. When it came to *Amigeerdong's* turn he fought against the ghost by throwing fire at it and was eventually victorious. Not only his image, but the weapons and tools that he used in the fight are frequently represented in the festival. Tshe mdo (Tshe Mdo, 2009) describes a similar festival (*lazi*) that took place in Qinghai Province

125

among an Amdo community. There the hero was named Amny Machen and his weapons were arrows—a key element of their ritual.

Newly painted *thangka* with figure of the hero.

Third is the role of the local *tusi* who like other *tusi* of the area had a multi-storeyed palace with a tower. The village of Qiong Shan is well known for its historic towers, which stand 9 or 10 storeys high (about 60m) (Frederique Darragon, 2006). The king of this area actually had two palaces, a winter palace in the river valley at Badi, and a summer palace at Qiong Shan which was the more elaborate of the two. This palace was burnt down in 1935 by the Red Army as they passed through the region on their long march. Although it was rebuilt it was later destroyed in the 1960s during the Cultural Revolution. The remains of the building now stand as a brown stone ruin demonstrating something of the former grandeur of the place. The remains of the tower stand some 9 storeys high and the walls mark out the significant area of the buildings.

Preparation for the Festival

Preparations for the festival had been underway for some time as it was necessary to gather materials for the ritual. According to tradition, everyone should wear new clothes for the festival, so many women had been busy making new clothes in the traditional style for their family members. The women of the region are famed for their beauty and the intricate needlework of their garments show this to the full, as well as the elaborate dress of the men.

Momo is the name of the local bread, but for the festival the loaves are formed into distinct shapes. This is similar to the practice found in other areas of the Tibetan world as mentioned with the *Losar* festival. These momos should be cooked in each household in Qiong Shan and in surrounding villages on the eve of the festival. This year it required the old women to teach the younger how to shape the momos, cook them in a pan and finally bake them in the ashes of the fire. The modelling of the bread was very important as each piece related to the story of the hero. The following is a description of how one older woman in Qiong Shan prepared her momos.

Momos that have been shaped are here cooking in the pan.

She first took pieces of dough and shaped them into representations of sheep. Platted strips were then pressed onto the shaped dough to make a depiction of the head and face. There were 12 equally sized figures of sheep and a larger one representing the leading ram. Other animal shapes that were modelled by the women included a pig, a pig with many young, a yak and an eagle. Weapons for the hero were also shaped which included a hammer, tongs, being the means by which he held the fire in his fight with the ghost, and a fork to fight the eagle. Bread was also shaped to represent the square tower of the palace as a symbolic representation of the king.

The old woman then took a piece of dough and shaped it into a large disk on which she pressed an elliptical mould dividing the circle into four segments. Then in each segment a round shape was placed. The shape is said to represent the earth and the ellipses the four directions. The ellipses represent what is called the "lock" of the earth, and when the occultation occurs the earth is "unlocked".

Two other important shapes that were formed represented the Sun and the Moon. The shape of the Sun was a circular disk with jagged edges, and a half circle represented the Moon. The number of momos depended upon the number of sons and daughters in a family. A moon-shaped momo should be given to every son, and a sun-shaped momo to every daughter. After the daughters marry and join husbands in other villages, the daughters used to come home for the festival when they are given their momo. Tradition says that they should stay for 28 days before a smaller festival was held when they eat their momo, but in practice the daughters eat their momo even if they returned home after a few days.

While the momos were being prepared in the various houses some of the old men were preparing a small shrine. These varied somewhat depending upon the dedication of the men to the festival and to their particular interpretation of the Bön tradition. Following is a description of the preparation made by one of the four old men.

First, he placed a small table in the corner of the main living room with the back facing east. Along the front of the table were placed seven brass bowls filled with rice. These could have been any odd number, but usually there are 5, 7 or 9. Behind these he placed an image of the Buddha. This was a large white porcelain figure of the "happy Buddha" found in many parts of China. He explained to me that he did not have a genuine Bön figure so he had to make do with this statue. To one side he placed 13 incense sticks in a dish. The most important aspect of the shrine which was centrally placed was a large circular metal tin marked with a Bön swastika with arms pointing in an anti-clockwise direction. Into this tin he placed the momo figures. The big ram was central and supported either side by 6 sheep. On each side of this line were placed the other figures. Then on top of the image of the large sheep was placed the shape of a sun and a moon.

In front of the shrine was then placed a thick mat on which to sit and beat a drum hanging from the roof. During late afternoon the old man commenced chanting from a Bön text. The completion of each section was marked by the clashing of cymbals and beating of the drum. For this old man the cymbals were particularly significant as he had kept them hidden for many years. The chanting continued for about 4 hours and went on well into the evening.

The early morning of 1st January 2007 was the predicted time for the occultation. However, light cloud and a nearly full moon meant that in the village the event could not be seen. A person coming from another area said that he had seen the star system and predicted that the occultation would occur about midnight. This was marked by the firing of a firework, which made a single loud bang that echoed through the valley.

The Festival

At this time of year, dawn does not break until about 8am and the high mountains cast dark shadows into the valley until about 10am when the bright sun brings warmth to the cold air. The main activities on the first day of the festival therefore commenced about 12.00 noon.

At this time of year the soil is very dry and a field that had not been prepared for cultivation had been chosen for the site. This field was on the west side of the village, but the exact position was not as important as the formation of the sacred space itself.

The four old men seated themselves on mats to the north side of the field. All the women were asked to leave the area, but they were allowed to watch from the nearby houses. As the old men faced south they began chanting while young men dug two holes in the centre of the field. Two trees had been cut, one larger than the other. Both had been prepared by strips of bark being cut from the four sides, which were said to represent north, east, south and west. Many of the men of the village then gathered to erect the tree, lowering it into the hole, and some pieces of wood were rammed around the tree to fix it firmly in place.

Brightly coloured cloths had been draped over the top of the tree before it was erected, and these blew in the light breeze. The old men explained that there should be five cloths in 5 different colours: 1) White representing snow and the east, 2) Red representing the lamas and the west, 3) Blue, the sky and the south. 4) Green, water and the north, 5) Yellow, the earth and the centre. When I pointed out that there were actually six cloths, I received a frank admission that a pink cloth had been bought by mistake and it had no meaning other than looking pretty.

When the tree was finally erected it could be seen that the lower branches had been cut. Ideally the fir tree should be left with 13 cusps of branches representing the 13 momos made in the form of sheep and the 13 incense sticks on the altar. In this case there were only 9 cusps of branches but this was regarded by the old men as being adequate.

The chant used during the ceremony was from a Bön text for peace that was named *The sacred mountains of Tibet* and included the names of important lamas. A second text was used to bring prosperity in the coming year. In the past the monks would have taken a more prominent role, but this year it was the four old lay men who led the chants. Two of them were especially noted for their spiritual powers.

The Communal Festival

The second day commenced with people making white smoke from the small shrines on the roofs of their houses. This was a sign that a festive gathering was going to occur on that day. Later loud music was broadcast through the modern speaker system echoing through the valley from the former king's palace. The villagers had made the area inside the palace clean and tidy, and erected a shrine at the north side of the square. In front of this was set the long table from which the dignitaries could watch the dancing. Some older women came early to claim good positions to sit and enjoy the day's activities.

A new thangka in traditional Tibetan style had been painted for the festival, and this was placed as a focus of the shrine. At the centre was a circle containing a representation of the hero, and above him was a smaller circle with a figure of the Buddha to express his higher status. The figures of the Sun and Moon were to the top right and left. Beneath the figure of the hero were the various symbols described earlier in the making of the momos. There were the 13 sheep, and various weapons and tools of the hero.

Fireworks announced the coming of people from the two villages higher up the valley. These are officially known as villages two and three. The people could be seen walking in long lines snaking down the valley all dressed in their finest costumes. From Qiong Shan (village one) two men wearing the costume of a white snow lion led the procession out to welcome the visitors. The people from villages 2 and 3 came in status order commencing with the older men, younger men, older women, women with no children and others. As they entered the courtyard of the palace, fireworks were again set off in the customary way of welcoming visitors and chasing away evil.

Dancing began almost immediately with the visitors dancing a guozhuang that are so well known in the region. Guozhuang comes from the Tibetan Guoxie which simply means singing and dancing in a circle. The Farmers' guozhuang begins with the men and women standing in two separate circles and singing in rotation while swaying and stamping their feet. Then their steps quicken and come to a stop often by shouting "Ya!".

In the afternoon a professional singing and dance group performed for the assembly. Almost half the young people in the group originated from the area and this had been organized by a local entrepreneur to entertain high level Party officials and tourists. Communal dancing commenced after the performance and continued into the darkness. Barley wine was warming in a large pan available for the dancers to partake during the intervals between the dances.

In the evening when darkness had come, the older men once again gathered at the site of the erected tree. The full moon brightly shone down to illuminate the area. While holding hands, the men circumambulated the tree in an anticlockwise direction chanting all the time. The chant was started by the oldest men and repeated by the rest of the circling group. The dance concluded with a shout as before.

Suddenly in the distance two fires were ignited by young men and their shouts echoed through the valley. Burning branches were then seen to be thrown from the hill into an empty field. The darkness made for a dramatic event. The older men ended their chanting and the young men put out their fires. Traditionally, it is said that the *tusi* sent a message to the boys to stop throwing fire and invited them to drink barley wine following which they danced.

The final day of the festival begins at about 11am with the chanting by the old men in the sacred area. The first tree was then lowered, care being taken to remove the cloths before they were dirtied from the dry soil. These were then placed on the smaller prepared tree that had been left to the side of the area. Suddenly there was a shout and the men rushed to break off the branches from the first tree. These branches were considered to bring prosperity in the coming year, and men handed these to their wives and placed sprays in their own headwear. The smaller tree was then carried with shouts into the palace where it was erected into a hole prepared in the centre of the dance area. Dancing once more began.

The old men dance around the trees before they are taken down.

Finally the elders offered chants and threw corn as a symbol of blessing and prosperity. The leaders of the university team were called forward to receive the thanks of the people for helping the village recommence the festival. People then sat in groups to eat lunch together. The festival was clearly coming to an end. The team from the university loaded their equipment into vehicles, and said goodbye to the people before walking back down the hill to the valley. The event had clearly been enjoyed by all, but it raised significant anthropological issues.

Authenticity or Invention?

As mentioned at the beginning, this particular New Year festival had been discontinued for some 54 years and so recovery of the tradition was based on the memories of four old men about events that had occurred more than half a century before. As the anthropologist would say, the "collective memory" of the community had been fragmented if not totally destroyed. This raises two significant questions: how accurately did the informants remember, and do the younger generation want to remember?

When asked how much they could remember, the oldest said he could remember very well as he was 33 years old when the festival was last held, and he had taken part in many of the festivals. When asked about specific incidents he was less certain. It would have been interesting to interview each of the old men separately to see exactly what they individually remembered about the festival in 1953, but this was not possible, nor actually worthwhile as they had already talked together much during the preparations. These discussions probably stimulated more personal memories, and helped reframe existing memories. In addition, some of these memories would not have been pleasant. One problem of doing such historical enquiry in China is that some people experienced such traumas that they have blanked much out of their memories. One man was visibly shaking as he drew out a set of cymbals that he had kept in hidden since the time of the Cultural Revolution in 1966 (Jun Jing, 1996).

When it comes to rituals and annual events, people often remember them more distinctly because they are repeated acts. The ritualized nature of such events enforces the memory even though it may be in a somewhat idealized manner. They become part of the category commonly expressed as "we have always done it this way"–the collective memory. Dances, songs and stories provide forms that allow a society to remember with surprising accuracy over many years and to pass on its traditions to younger generations.

It was however acknowledged by our informants that the specific meaning of many of the symbols had been lost. These were known only by the "secretary" of the king who arranged the actual events. The last man to hold this role had died some years ago and with him, our informants all agreed, had died the ancient meanings. One example of this related to some stones now placed under a single fir tree in the field south of Qiong Shan. One stone had markings in the form of the

Pleiades (M45), but today no one knows how this is specifically related to the festival, if at all. There was also another stone which looks as though it has been shaped into a phallus. Once again, the meaning had been lost. Both these stones had been in the palace and were moved under the tree following the palace fire. The tree itself is an enigma. It stands in splendid isolation in the centre of the field and all that can be remembered was that it had once been struck by lightning so that the top of the tree had been destroyed.

Although the four old men could remember the outward forms of the festival, and some of the symbolic meaning, the traditional authority was lost with the removal of the *tusi*. The 1950s and 1960s were difficult times for people in China and most people were merely struggling to stay alive rather than bothering with such activities. Nevertheless, the festival did not completely come to a halt, and some elements continued quietly in the homes of some the villagers. Families continued to bake momos and construct the shrine in their homes, but all the communal activities ended with the departure of the king.

Even with the making of the *momos* there was a lack of clarity as to their symbolic meaning. The way in which the momos were made was remembered by the older women, but when asked about the meaning of the shapes there was little clarity. Why were the momos given to the men in the shape of the moon, and that for women in the shape of the sun? The answer was that this is how it had always been done and it was a way of distinguishing men and women. The momos were also a way of asking the gods to give them a happy prosperous society.

The old men were aware that they could not merely reproduce what had happened in 1952, but they were adamant that "there were not many changes". There was however one major difference in that there was no longer a king and his palace is now a ruin. The *tusi* presided over the festival, and this year they had decided that it should be the old men and village leaders who would have this responsibility. The smaller second tree should have been brought to the king, so they decided it should be brought to the palace. The men felt that the *dongko*, the large prayer wheel at the gateway of the palace, in some way represented the king. Other innovations were the invitation to the local Party officials and the performance by a specially invited professional dance troop. These illustrate the conscious need to relate to the contemporary situation, and the need to explore the tourist potential of the event.

This raises the issue of the authenticity of the festival. As Smith writes: "By *authentic* we usually mean that something is genuine and original, that it can be certified by evidence, or remains true to a tradition." (Smith, 2003) Certainly every attempt was made to ensure the festival remained true to the tradition remembered by the old men as it existed until 50 years ago, but some changes were consciously introduced. Even with no disruption, changes would have occurred though more likely on an incremental scale. What was important for the people themselves was that they saw the festival as a genuine continuation and not a fabrication. *Authenticity* is important if the event is going to have any significant role in establishing social identity, but it is also important with regards to tourist potential.

The people saw the festival as something particularly belonging to them. It was a unique expression of their social identity, and for a community seeing many of its young people move away to the cities it had great significance. The festival has the potential of being a time of family gathering like the Spring Festival among the Han Chinese or *Losar* among Tibetans. If the festival continued and was accepted by the younger generation, it could be an encouragement for the young people to return home and participate in communal activities that would affirm their social identity. This New Year festival could be one means by which people of the area could retain their identity in the midst of the social changes affecting modern China and this region of Sichuan. As Lambek and Antze write, "In order to constitute themselves, nations need to discover (or construct) a past, a collective memory." (Antze, P. & Lambek, 1996:11). For the people of the area, the accuracy of the festival was not as important as the fact that it came from the memories of their people, and so was adopted as a collective memory by those who participated.

The myth of the hero that is central to the narrative illustrates something of the ideas of Eliade. The timeless hero fights against the forces of evil that continually attack and weaken the people, and he is victorious. The Rgyalrong people have faced many conflicts and defeats in the last two centuries. Their history has been written by historians as if they are merely part of the Tibetan minority nationality of modern China. Their mythical hero is an expression of a desire to reclaim at least some small part of their culture.

Finally, there is the question of the role of the anthropologist. Certainly, the methods of anthropology were valuable in providing a holist perspective on the local situation and a culturally sensitive approach to the interviews with the many informants. Perhaps it was participant observation that had the greatest impact. The people were delighted to see the anthropologist, his wife and some of the team dressed in traditional costume taking part in the dances. This came even to the point that the anthropologist was given the honour of leading one of the dances! This was certainly not due to his dance skills. What seemed to be important was that he was not just behind the cameras trying to record some exotic ritual, but was participating with them in the event. The festival was not an enactment of a historic event, but was an expression of contemporary life. What seemed to be more important to the people was that someone from outside their valley, and even from outside China was willing to participate. Their festival suddenly had a place, no matter how small in the global expression of human cultures.

Continuity and Change

Questions remain as to whether the festival will continue and whether the young people adopt it as a particular expression of their own unique identity as *Rgyalrongwa*. The villages do now have a photographic record of the festival in which they participated in January 2007 and again for a second time in December 2007. The personal memories of the four old men have now been expressed in ritual and documented visually. In this way it is hoped that it has become something of the collective memory of the society.

However in the winter of 2008, the third year of the event, the public celebration of the festival did not take place. There are various reasons for this of which one was the absence of funding and participation of the team from Chengdu. There were also changes in the leadership of the village and various social tensions. One of the four old men also died during the year, so out of respect some people felt that it was not a good time to dance. Some local people also began to question the value of renewing the festival after all these years. They had said that no one could be interested in the ancient festivals of a small community in the west of China.

The festival recommenced in the Decembers of 2009, 2010 and 2011. As would be expected there were some incremental changes; some additions, omissions and modifications. For example, in 2011 there were some small additions. First, on the shrine dedicated to the hero was an additional item in the form of a rod with a dragon form. The dragon represents kingship in the region with kings classed as having one, two or three dragons. The highest king with three dragons was based in Kangding the capital of the ancient Kham kingdom. Here in Badi the king had only two dragons. This dragon rod was only recently discovered and was incorporated into the festival. The second dragon rod remains lost. Here is another indication of the important role of the tusi in the life of the community.

Secondly, at the end of the festival the leading old man led the people in a prayer that was traditionally made for the tusi. This was something that was only done in the private quarters of the tusi in ancient times, but now it was recited publically.

Thirdly, the pink cloth that was in the first year added by mistake was in 2011 was placed on the second tree, not the first. The significance of the five colours therefore remains on the first tree - a small but notable change.

Some things were however omitted. For example, there was no procession down the hill from second village. Village three had previously given up attending the festival as they felt they were too far away (about 1 hour on foot) and also felt they were populous enough to have their own ritual. In 2011, the reason that villagers from the second village did not process down together was simply because notification of the festival came so late they had no time to prepare. There was therefore no welcoming dragon dance.

These are small changes that you would expect to occur with any festival as it adapts year-on-year. More significant was the decline in numbers attending the festival. Most of the people who danced were elderly. Most of their children had migrated to the towns and cities of Sichuan to dance and sing or cook in Tibetan restaurants. The timing of the festival is something of a problem as it occurs four weeks before the all-important Chinese Spring holiday and so migrant workers and students are unable to return for the festival. In 2011, the local primary school in Qiong Shan had only 18 students, and soon closed with the children being relocated to the boarding school in Badi. The village will therefore become increasingly one of old people and the children will not be there to learn the traditional dances.

Some people had hoped that the festival might become a tourist attraction with commercial potential. One man has set his home up as an excellent guesthouse for tourists, and some do find their way up to the village. However, winter is not a popular time for Chinese or foreign tourists to come to the region as snow and ice make the roads difficult and dangerous. Traditional dances and rituals could be moved to a different time of the year, but this can hardly be done with a festival known as one for the New Year.

It is still uncertain whether the public expression of the New Year festival will continue to be revived. This depends on whether the people see this as "usable memory"—to use Connerton's expression. For the younger generations now living in the towns and cities of Sichuan, Qiong Shan is far away and festivals there seem to have little significance in New China. Perhaps in this case, the young people will not see this as usable memory but only a village in which their ancestors once lived. Perhaps the only thing that the project will have achieved is having made a video recording that parents can one day show to their children or grandchildren, and the next generation of anthropologists will be able to discuss.

11 Folk Religion

This is the first of three chapters exploring religious change among the Rgyalrongwa. Early western writers on Tibetan religion often used the term Bön to refer to a wide variety of allegedly pre-Buddhist and non-Buddhist elements. While there are some grounds for using the term Bön for the early religion of Tibet, there is little reason to make this association today. I am therefore following Geoffrey Samuel's argument that after the ninth century A.D. Bön and Bönpa refer exclusively to the religious orders of Bön and its adherents. (Samuel, 1993, 12 & 176). This order is similar in form and nature to the clerical orders of Tibetan Buddhism apart from the claim that their teaching derives from the pre-Buddhist master Shenrab Mibo rather than Buddha Sakyamuni. Today modern Bön religion has what Samuel calls "shamanistic" and "clerical" elements in a way similar to those of modern Tibetan Buddhism. These three chapters will therefore look at modern folk-religion ("shamanistic") together with modern Bön and modern Tibetan Buddhism both of which are "clerical" in structure.

The term folk religion is therefore used to describe that group of complex religious and magical beliefs and practices that fall outside organized clerical religion, and generally lack written documents or systematic teaching. Tucci (Tucci, 1980, 163-212) also uses the term "folk religion" while Stein (Stein, 1972, 191) prefers the more nebulous expression "the nameless religion". As mentioned previously, folk religion is closely associated with pre-Buddhist Tibetan cults that include local gods considered to reside on mountains, methods of defence against evil forces, divination and healing. These practices constitute what Bönpo scholars later refer to as the "Bön of Cause" (*gyui Bön)* as distinct from the "Bön of Effect" (*drebui Bön).*

The term "folk" was first used in this sense in 1956 by Robert Redfield in his book *Peasant Society and Culture.* He argued that peasant society is not autonomous, but an aspect of the civilisation of which it is a part. He therefore distinguishes two concepts—the great and the little traditions, which he describes as: "Two currents of thought and action, distinguishable, yet ever flowing into and out of each other." (Redfield, 1956). Later Obeyesekere (Obeyesekere, 1963) commented that because cultures are integrated it is impossible to clearly distinguish the great and little traditions. The term "great tradition" is useful in describing the intellectual thought and interests of civilizations and groups of individuals who promote those interests, which we have here called the beliefs and practices belonging to religious orders. The "little tradition" by contrast is the whole culture of the peasant society, which is linked with the great tradition through common idiom. These common cultural idioms establish channels of communication between the two traditions, and link peasant society with the greater tradition.

In modern China, there are five officially recognized religions: Buddhism, Islam, Daoism, Roman Catholic Christianity and Protestant Christianity. Confucian belief is now considered a distinct school of philosophy and statues of Confucius find pride of place in most university campuses. Everything outside these five religions is classed a *superstition* and so is considered unimportant. It is argued that scientific development and education will eventually remove such ignorant beliefs and practices from society.

Today, one can look at the major religious and magical traditions in the Rgyalrong region as being threefold: atheist, organized religion and folk religion. As will be shown, people do not necessarily see these as being mutually exclusive. One tradition can be important in one context and another in a different context. A local Communist Party member can therefore happily go to a temple and prostrate before an image of the local mountain deity whilst acknowledging the atheistic teaching of the Party.

Mountain gods

To the Rgyalrongwa the world is inhabited not only by humans and animals, but also by countless other beings that might be described as gods, spirits and ghosts. These are found in what Wellens writing of the Premi calls the "invisible dimension of the natural world", which avoids words like "supernatural" whilst implying some "other worldly" quality (Wellens & Project Muse, 2010: 132).

One of the most ancient traditions of Tibetan belief relates to local deities (*yulha*). Throughout Tibet it is believed that each family has a local god as does each geographical region. These gods can easily be offended, and their anger can be dangerous. It is therefore necessary to keep on good terms with the local gods to secure good fortune in the world and everyday life. The local deities are associated with the most notable mountains in the region on which they are believed to reside. Each mountain god possessed his own territory and is in charge of particular local affairs (Xie Jisheng & Jisheng, 2001).

Around each god has sprung up a complex system of myths, legends, sacrificial rites and ceremonies (Jisheng, 2001). One example concerns the mountain deity Murdo (*Dmu rdo*). During the time of the Qing Dynasty (1644-1912), over an eight year period, the Qing soldiers fought the Tibetan forces, but continually suffered defeat. Many more Qing soldiers were sent until the Qing were close to victory. At this point, the Tibetan soldiers offered *bsang* to Murdo and asked him for help. It is said that the sky suddenly grew dark and Murdo appeared on a black horse, took out soldiers from his robe, scattered them on the battlefield, and the Qing army was soon defeated.

One important set of rituals relates to stone cairns that are found at the highest point of a passé or other places believed to be near to the abode of the deity. It is customary for a traveller to carry a stone up an ascent to the cairn and place it on the cairn with an invocation such as "The gods are victorious!". These cairns are called the castles of the gods, but the gods are expected to reside there without causing trouble in return for being provided with a home and regular offerings. The cairns are often decorated with coloured prayer flags attached to sticks projecting from the stones. Flat stones inscribed with mantras are often added to the pile in order to bring blessing as a result of the movement of the person passing the site.

In the Rgyalrong area a large white stone is frequently placed on the top of the pile. It is necessary to restate that in this area many of the villages are built high up on the side of the main valley and are only accessible by climbing the narrow path that zigzags up the hillside. This climb may take several hours and the loose stones do not make for an easy climb especially if the person is carrying a load. The placing of a stone on the cairn is often just a token of gratitude for a safe climb.

Another common ritual is the circumambulation of the local mountain out of respect to the deity of the mountain. For example, two of my students on returning from university in Chengdu were required by their family to make such a circumambulation of the hill behind their home. The regular offerings are known as *sang*, which consist of burning incense and the offering of prayer flags. Recitation of the names of regional and local deities is also a common feature. *Sang* do not merely have a protective function, but are hoped to create positive influences for the good fortune of all. These may be performed by an individual, family or even a whole village.

The offering of white smoke is also a common ritual performed by the Rgyalrongwa. This is usually made each day in the early hours before cooking. The oldest male of a household climbs to the roof of his house and there in a small fireplace he would light a fire with twigs of various sorts. White smoke then rises from the chimney high into the sky as he makes a short prayer.

It is common for the patriarch of the family to carry some of the smoking embers into the main rooms of the house as a blessing. Members of the family would wave the smoke onto themselves as a symbol of blessing (Huarui & Dongshi, 2001). This is performed on the primary school children before they begin what could be a long and somewhat dangerous walk to their school. When children move to residential secondary schools in the towns this practice stops, but when they return home at the weekends it quickly becomes a part of their lives again. This simple ritual well illustrates the two totally different ways of life many of the children experience: atheistic at school and religious at home.

High mountains can take on special importance. Mount Murdo near the town of Danba in the centre of the Rgyalrong region has been mentioned in previous chapters because it has become one of the most important mountains in the area. The name Murdo (Dmu rdo) means the "Stone of Satan" and worship is therefore offered to appease his wrath. These high mountains are seen as the residence of the deity of the local territory (*yul-lha*), and in addition many were chosen as *gter-gnas*, "places of treasures". They were considered to be suitable places for the concealment of religious texts (*gter*) at the time of the persecution of early Bön, or for future purposes in the case of Nyingma School. Both traditions maintain that these events took place in the eighth century A.D. A long list of such sites is recorded in Bön texts, and these are often described as suitable for hermits to dwell. If a site is designated as *gter-gnas*, the deity then becomes *gter-bdag or gter-srung*, meaning the guardian of the treasury". When texts are discovered, the location becomes even more sacred, but to obtain the status of *gnas-ri* for the mountain this must be instituted by a religious man. This involves the marking out of the footpath around the mountain for circumambulation in the presence of the public. It involves the identification of various places on the path considered to have been former dwellings of religious saints. The last day of the marking out of the route is designated for the annual celebration. Finally a guide is written for the holy mountain (Samten G Karmay, 1996).

In the Bön tradition Mt Murdo is known through two "text-revellers": Sangye lingpa and his disciple Kun-grol grags-pa (b. 1700). In 1727 Sangye lingpa was travelling to Central Tibet from Khyungpo in Kham, when news reached him of political unrest in Lhasa. He therefore went to Kongpo where he received prophetic signs indicating that he would be able to reveal sacred texts from Mt Murdo. In 1728 while still in Kongpo he met a monk named Blo-Ldan snyingpo who was related to the *tusi* of Gechizha (*dGe-shes-tsa*) that is to the east of modern Danba. The monk became his disciple and the *tusi* invited Sangye lingpa to visit his kingdom. After visiting various places he arrived at the monastery bKra-shis smin-grol-gling in Nyag-rong where he met two men who were to become his chief disciples, one of which was a prince of the royal family.

Sangye lingpa continued to receive visions to go to Mt Murdo, which he believed to have been a place visited by the Bönpo master Dran-pa nam-mkha in the eighth century. He arrived in Rgyalrong early in 1731 and was welcomed by the tusi of Gechizha. One month later he set out with five assistants for the cave to the south of Mt Murdo where he received various prophecies in a dream. In this cave he found various *gter* objects. Finally after various setbacks and special rituals he established the route for the pilgrimage around Mt Murdo.

Rgyalrongwa celebrate what they call the "birthday of Mt Murdo" on the 10th day of the seventh month (the horse month) in the Tibetan calendar. This day usually falls in August, but as the pilgrimage takes 3 or 4 days pilgrims come four days earlier. Murdo is the highest mountain in the region at 4820 metres, and has four small peaks if viewed from the south side. Pilgrims perform the circumambulation either in a clockwise or anticlockwise direction depending on their religious affiliation. Buddhists journey with their right hand towards the mountain and Bön with their left hand. They often simply use a hand gesture to show which direction they go round a sacred place, so identifying their allegiance.

Liu (Liu Yaling, 2009) says that there are three different routes. The shortest passes around the temple of Dmu rdo and the vicinity; the second goes only to the summit of the mountain, and the third is all the way around the foot of the mountain without ascending it. It might seem strange that people walk to the temple when a road runs close by it, but the pilgrims would say that unless some effort was involved in the pilgrimage, the Buddha and the mountain god would not think that they were sincere and so would not grant their petitions.

A small temple called *Murdo lhakhang* is located on the southern side of the mountain next to the Tsanchu River which flows towards Danba. The old temple was destroyed during the Cultural Revolution, and was rebuilt through the initiative of a Buddhist monk in the 1980s (Samten G Karmay, 1996). Karmay described the temple following a visit in 1993 as having three storeys with a Chinese styled roof. This has been improved over the years and in 2010 it was undergoing further renovation which was completed at the end of 2010.

On the ground floor surrounding the outer part of the temple is a set prayer wheels. After circumambulating the hall and spinning the prayer wheels, the visitors enter the hall and prostrate themselves before the image of the mountain deity and ask for his blessing. The statue of the mountain deity shows him riding on a horse and holding a sword in his right hand – see following figure.

Statue of the deity of Mt Murdo.

A stairway on the outside allows one to climb to the second floor where there is a shrine room containing images of various bodhisattvas.

On the top (third) floor is a smaller chamber containing a statue of Gautama Buddha. The face of the statue looks more like that of a Rgyalrong man rather than Han Chinese. The three-storeys illustrate the local-global perspective. On the ground floor is the deity of the local mountain, then comes the bodhisattvas that are various expressions of the Buddha and finally at the top is the Buddha himself.

Outside the temple, but still in the temple ground, is a large rock on top of which is a stone cairn dedicated to Mt Murdo. Steps allow visitors to climb up to the cairn with joss sticks purchased from the stores outside the complex. There they perform a simple *sang* purification ritual by burning the joss sticks, burning paper offerings and making prostrations. Lines of prayer flags decorate the mound. A monk is usually available to help the visitors if requested.

The temple complex has been extended over recent years. In the wooded area next to the temple and beside the river there is now a large stupa and also a small shrine. This shrine contains a large rock on which rest two figures said to represent the disciples of a bodhisattva. This stone is said to have been used by the mountain god in his sling to destroy the forces of evil in the area.

The cult of Murdo shows that dogmatic differences are ignored. Buddhists circumambulate the temple clockwise whereas Bön pilgrims circumambulate in an anticlockwise direction and they happily greet each other as they meet in the middle at the rear. Similarly many Rgyalrongwa join the annual pilgrimage and as they journey around the mountain, they greet each other. This is a Rgyalrong festival to which families come to ask blessing for various situations. One family I met were planning to undertake the pilgrimage so that their youngest son would do better at college in the following year. As Karmay has written of the annual pilgrimage "Indeed, it is a unique occasion for manifesting their religious identities among themselves as well as a means of expressing their cultural differences from the Chinese." (Karmay, 1996:14).

La and the gods

Another important concept in Tibetan folk religion is that of *la* or "life force". It is not related to Buddhism, but it is a common notion among shamanistic societies (Burnett, 2005). For example, it corresponds to the concept of *khwan* discussed by Stanley Tambiah in his study of the Northeast Thai (Tambiah 1970). It is probably therefore a pre-Buddhist belief that has continued until today. Samuel defines the *la* as "a spirit-essence or life-principle residing in the body, and particularly in the earlier period, it was seen as connected also with one or more external objects. Such external objects or resting places of the *la* might he hills, lakes or groves of trees." (Samuel, 1993:187). As with many concepts of folk-religion, the ideas concerning *la* are not easily expressed in a coherent or consistent way. It is therefore more easily seen in everyday beliefs, ritual and even songs.

One notion of the *la* is that it can leave the body of the individual, and when this happens the person is left weakened and exposed to harm. Similar effects can occur if the external resting place is damaged or destroyed. A lama may be called on to perform a ceremony to recall the wandering *la*, and restore the individual to health. Such rituals are commonly performed with young children among the Tibetans as described by others (Lakhu, Libu, Stuart, C.K. & Roche, 2009).

Both Stein and Tucci argue that the concept of *la* is closely linked to the local gods in their role as personal protective deities of *gowe lha* (Stein, 1972; Tucci, 1980). *Gowe lha* are a set of five gods who are said to be born at the same time as the child. Scholars have gathered various lists but these vary. Generally they consist of a "god of life" with its seat in the heart, a male god in the right armpit, a female deity in the left armpit, *drabla* ("enemy god") at the right shoulder and *yullha* ("god of the locality") at the crown of the head.

The concept is also expressed in connection with the protection of a household. Tucci writes about *p'olha* (male god) that normally has a shrine on the roof where incense is burned. *P'olha* is associated with the men of the household and with the external defence of the house.

Molha (female god) has a shrine inside the house in the central pillar. It is concerned with the well-being of the family and particularly the female members. Other deities look over the hearth (*t'ablha*) and the storehouse (*bangdzod lha*).

The complement of these local gods are the hosts of malevolent spirits that are a constant threat to life and property. Much ritual activity is directed towards them both at the folk level and that of the formal traditions. These spirits are of many forms and lay people are more concerned with the protection they give rather than detailed classification, whereas monastic scholars and lamas tend to be more concerned with their classification as it is they who have to deal with those who are afflicted.

It is for the purpose of protection that one has to keep on good terms with the local gods. These gods can protect an individual, family or village, but if so inclined can either withdraw their protection or release the spirits in their own retinue to cause harm. Thus most of the New Year rituals have elements to do with repelling evil forces from the area, as was discussed in the previous chapter on the New Year ritual in Badi.

Furer-Haimendorf in his description of the Sherpas makes a distinction between malevolent spirits and two other sources of evil: *norpa* or ghosts, and *pem* or witches (Furer-Haimendorf 1964: 241-256). Death is a major time of crisis and there is great need for protection against the spirit of the dead person and the risk of it failing to find another body and so become an evil ghost. It is the Buddhist monks and lamas who carry out the mortuary rituals to help a successful rebirth as was discussed in chapter 8. In contrast witches are people who cause misfortune to come on other people, and as in most societies witches are considered to be mainly women.

The importance of local gods, malevolent spirits, ghosts and witches vary between communities and even individuals. They are however an important part of the symbolic language of the Tibetans to describe the practical concerns about their lives and households. Although the lamas and the Buddhist Tantric deities represent a source of superior power to the local gods, they are not directly concerned with local issues and ordinary life.

Divination and Omens

Another common set of beliefs and practices in folk religions is that of divination and omens. Throughout Tibet, divination (*mo*) and the reading of omens (*tendrel*) are common. Divination provides a means to find answers to questions of misfortune, and this is especially significant with the Buddhist connection of cause and effect through the karmic link. As all things are connected, it is possible for a skilful observer to read the signs and discern if the date or time is auspicious. For example, a Rgyalrong farmer may come out of his house in the morning and hear the sound of monks chanting in the monastery nearby, and this would bring him a sense of wellbeing. If, however, he comes out and sees a black cat in the corn or a crow cries above his head, he may consider that the day is not auspicious and so decide to change the task he had planned for the day.

In addition to reading the signs (*tendrel*), there are specific techniques of divination to discern if a situation is auspicious. Is it a good time to undertake building a new house, to erect a prayer flag, conclude a marriage or set out to trade? Some of these methods are very general and can be performed by anyone, lay or monk. They could be as simple as counting the beads on a rosary. However many other techniques can only be performed by a monk or lama on behalf of the laity. As will be discussed in the chapter on Gelugpa monasteries, this is often one of the special skills in which a monk can train. Methods used by the lamas include mechanical techniques such as the casting of divining-arrows or divining-dice, and some lamas are believed to have spiritual powers that enable them to divine without the use of any specific apparatus.

Astrology is also a common phenomenon in the Tibetan region where it combines techniques from both India and China. This is expert knowledge only associated with the monastery and lamas. Astrology can determine whether a particular day is auspicious for a specific activity. The most spectacular form of divination is that of the spirit-medium when a lama is possessed by one of the major protective deities of the monastery.

Spirit-mediums are found in villages throughout the Tibetan region. These are usually men and in the Rgyalrong area function as local shaman like the *shibi* of the Qiang. They are usually possessed by mountain deities, and are often involved with healings relating to the calling back of the *la* that may have been lost from a person. One of their most important tools in this practice is the one-sided drum, which is common among many of the Siberian shaman.

Another common figure in the Rgyalrong area is the fortune-teller (Chinese: *suan ming xian sheng*). Every New Year the family would invite the fortune-teller to come to their home and tell them their fortune for the coming year. Knowing their birth date and after consulting two books, he would draw up a square matrix into which he would place the various members of the family. He would then subsequently be able to give advice to each of them on various aspects of their life and behaviour.

First, what foods they should eat or avoid during the coming year. For example, during one year the older sister in the family I knew was told to avoid eating fish, while the younger sister was told to avoid eating chicken.

Second, particular places they should avoid. A person may be told to avoid water or any houses that are being constructed. This seems to result from a danger of harm resulting from being in one or other of these locations.

Third, the fortune-teller will give advice on particular auspicious colours that the person should wear during the year. One informant was told that she should wear red or yellow during the current year, and so she ensured that she always wore at least one article of clothing with these colours.

Fourth, advice could be given on appropriate speech and behaviour. Usually this is that a younger person should always speak respectfully and humbly to an older person.

Finally, there is always an element of specific predictions and warnings. For example, a person may be told that during the coming year they may lose some money or have problems with their education. As with horoscopes in all societies there is an element of ambiguity, which allows the client to apply the words to their own particular situation.

Contemporary Religion

Contemporary religion in the Rgyalrong region can therefore be seen as complex and diverse. The atheistic teaching which is common to the school curriculum throughout China does not deter students from going to the monastery or temple to request a blessing. Neither does it deter lower level officials of the CCP from taking part in celebrations or even going on pilgrimage. These practices are conveniently placed in the official category of superstitions rather than religion. There is therefore a dual worldview: one relates to the government, science and education; one relates to the village, family beliefs and requests to the local gods for help and blessings. Terwiel in his study of village Buddhism in Thailand has made the useful distinction between what he calls "syncretistic religion", which is similar to what we have here been calling folk religion, and "compartmentalised religion". (Terwiel, 1994).

During the Cultural Revolution (1966-76) public expression of religion was banned in China and temples were destroyed. As we have seen among the Rgyalrong, temples were closed and festivals were banned. As with the New Year festival in Badi, the public aspect was banned and only recently recommenced, but many practices still continued privately in the homes of the local people. This helped retain the "compartmentalised" perspective of religion.

It is most likely that ancient Bön ideas and practices were brought by the people in their migration from western Tibet. In the ethnic corridor in which they settled they encountered many other religious practices such as those from the Qiang and many Daoist ideas from the Han Chinese. With the emergence of Buddhism as the state religion in Lhasa some Bön monks may have sought refuge in the region. With the establishment of New Bön in the 12th century this resulted in the establishment of Bön monasteries that were accepted by the *tusi* rulers as the state religion of their kingdom. Slowly, Gelugpa brought about the conversion of some of the northern *tusi*. This resulted in the three traditions mentioned at the beginning of this chapter.

In western society there has been a gradual process of secularization in society. Beliefs and rituals that were once strongly held have often become quaint local customs that attract the tourists. Among the Rgyalrong folk religion is still strong even 60 years after liberation in 1950.

12 Bön Religion

In the historical account of the region written in chapter 1 it was mentioned that the earliest religion developed into modern day Bön. It was only about 400 years ago that the dGelugpa ("yellow hat") Buddhism entered the region of Rgyalrong, and for many years it made little advance against the existing Bön tradition. Eventually four of the northern *tusi* accepted the dGelugpa, but the southern region has generally remained strongly Bön even until recent times.

The central region around Badi illustrates the local expression of Bön as well as the growing influence of dGelugpa. Badi was the residence of the local *tusi* who had his winter palace in the main valley at Badi, and a summer palace at Qiong Shan in the hills to the west. Badi currently consists of 21 hamlets and one source lists 28 temples in Danba County, 10 belonging to *Bönpa* ("Black Hat"), 8 temples to *Nyingma* ("Red Hat"), 7 temples to *dGelugpa* ("Yellow Hat") and 3 are of mixed traditions.

History of Bön

The Bön tradition states that Shenrab Mibo brought Bön to the ancient kingdom of Zhang-zhung in western Tibet. (Chogyal Namkai Norbu & D. Rossi, 2013). This is the kingdom that Rgyalrong tradition speaks of as being the realm of the queen who sent some of her people east to the gold river. If such a migration happened, this would indeed imply that Rgyalrongwa brought Bön with them from their homeland.

As mentioned in the previous chapter, the figure of Shenrab Mibo has acquired many of the characteristics and stories associated with the Indian tradition of Shakyamuni Buddha. This suggests a Buddhist influence earlier than that generally assumed to have come from northwest India in the seventh century during the reign of Songtse Gampo. A transmission through Persia prior to the seventh century A.D. is also not improbable as Alexander the Great had connected Greece with India centuries earlier resulting in a flourishing Greco-Buddhist culture in what is now Afghanistan and Pakistan. The early history of this region is still a subject of research and on-going debate.

It is not clear when Zhang-zhung was actually conquered, but it was most likely in the first half of the seventh century. (Chogyal Namkai Norbu & D. Rossi, 2013). The records of the Chinese Tang Dynasty place this in the reign of Songtsen Gampo (617-649) for they say that in AD 634 Zhang-zhung and various Qiang tribes "submitted to him". Following this, Songtsen Gampo united with Zhang-zhung to defeat the Azha or Tuyuhun, and then conquered two more tribes of Qiang before threatening Songzhou with his army. He then sent an envoy with gifts of gold and silk to the Chinese emperor to ask for a Chinese princess in marriage and, when the emperor refused, he attacked Songzhou. According to the Tang annals, he finally retreated and apologised and later the emperor granted his request, but the histories written in Tibet all say that the Tibetan army defeated the Chinese, and that the Tang emperor delivered a bride under threat of force. It seems as if Songtsen Gampo married a Nepalese princess in 632, and Princess Wenchang, daughter of the Emperor Tang Taisong in 641. This was the time that Buddhism was approaching a highpoint, and it is therefore not surprising that Songtsen Gampo adopted Buddhism as the state religion. Bön was officially abolished around AD 785 (Karmay, 1972, 118), and it is likely that at this time many Bönpo (Bön practitioners) decided to move to the frontiers of the Tibetan empire.

From 785 until 1017 very little is known about Bön, and then in 1017 an ancient text was (re-)discovered by gShen-chen Klu-dga (995-1035), which stimulated a revival of Bön. gShen-chen Klu-dga is best known in Bön as a "treasure revealer" (*gter-ston*), and the argument continues as to whether he made a genuine discovery as he claims, or he rewrote a Buddhist text. (D. A. N. Martin, 1996). These texts assert that Yungdrung, "eternal" Bön was founded by the Buddha Tonpa Shenrab Miwoche who is said to have lived 18,000 years ago in the land of Olmo Lung Ring, to the west of modern Tibet. Miwoche was considered to be one of the many manifestations of the Buddha prior to the manifestation of Shakyamuni Buddha. Miwoche's teaching was similar to the Dharma of Shakyamuni and this he taught to the people of Zhang-zhung who had previously only practiced shamanistic Bön. These texts "discovered" by gShen-chen Klu-dga helped form a fully organized Bön religion with many similarities to Buddhism. As a result the hostility between Bön and Buddhism lessened, and Shakyamuni Buddha was adopted by Bönpo as one of the deities who guide individuals. In the 14th century the Bön canon was codified by Nyame Sherab Gyaltsen, the first abbot of Menri Monastery, but it is likely that the process began earlier. Similar changes were happening in Nyingma, Kagyu and Sakya orders who were also trying to reorganize themselves in order to compete with the dominant influence of the dGelug order.

Kvaerne (Kværne, 1995) therefore argues that Bön has three distinct aspects: (1) the pre-Buddhist religious practices of Tibetans that focus on the personage of a divine king; (2) a syncretistic religion that emerged in Tibet during the 10th and 11th centuries, with strong shamanistic traditions and Buddhist ideas and practices; (3) a vast and amorphous body of popular beliefs.

In the 14th century a new expression of Bön emerged that is sometimes called "New Bön". At this time some Bön teachers claimed to have discovered *termas* related to Padmasambhava. New Bön is primarily practiced in the eastern regions of Tibet: Amdo and Kham. Although the practices of New Bön vary to some extent from Yungdrung Bön, the practitioners of New Bön still honour the Abbot of Menri Monastery as the leader of their tradition.

With the birth of the Fifth Dali Lama in 1617, Tibet was divided into several competing political and religious factions. In 1641 all of Tibet came under the overlordship of the Mongols who adopted dGelug tradition, and made the Fifth Dalai Lama head of state (Samten G Karmay, 2005). One of the most influential figures in the movement of the New Bön tradition in Rgyalrong in the eighteenth century was Kun grol grags pa (b.1700, hereafter called Kun grol) whose mentor was Sangs rgyas gling pa (1705-1735), a mystic and gter ston from Tsha ba rong in Kham. Sangs rgyas urged Kun grol to work with him on the revival of the Bön tradition in Rgyalrong.

The practical outcome of these developments is that in the Rgyalrong region one can identify a wide range of practitioners within the Bön tradition. At one end there are lay shamans who are called upon for divination, and at the other are monks who are resident at large monasteries that are similar to those of the dGelugpa tradition. Between these are smaller, family based temples and monasteries that have been little influenced by dGelugpa teaching apart from the fact that they wear ruby-red robes.

Temples and monasteries

The smaller temples vary greatly in character, but have many similar outward characteristics. They are usually positioned outside the main village in some auspicious site sometimes near the burial site for the village. Various physical manifestations can mark out a particular location. For example one local monk was eager to point out to me a rock that had a distinctive depression in the shape of a human foot. The monk claimed this was a place where a person of great spiritual power once stood.

The simple building that may make up the shrine room usually contains a few sacred images that provide the focus for worship. There is often a small room in which the local priest will sleep. He, for it is usually a man, is often illiterate and has learned the rituals from his father. These smaller shrines in the mountain villages are usually associated with larger monasteries in the river valley where larger numbers of the people live and work. To the outsider these monasteries do not look very different from those of the Buddhist tradition, but one can immediately note a difference in the direction of circumambulation around a holy place.

The Bön Canon is in two parts, the *Kangyur* and *Tengyur* (Kvaerne, 1974). The Kangyur in turn is divided into four parts: "mDo" (Sutras), "Bum" (Prajnaparamita), "rGyud" (Tantras) and "mDzod" (Treasure-House) that contain texts dealing with higher forms of meditation. All the texts of the *Kangyur* are *Ka* or teachings of the three dimensions (*ku, kaya*) of Tonpa Shenrab. These include 62 volumes of *sutra* and 91 volumes of *Prajnaparamita* texts; 18 volumes of tantric texts including the *Ma Gyud* (Mother Tantra), *Sherab Chamma, Sidpe Gyalmo*, and four volumes of Dzogchen *texts*. One of these four is the *Zhang-zhung Nyen Gyu* (The Oral Transmission of Zhang-zhung) the oldest and most important *Dzogchen* tradition and meditation system in Bön based on a series of "secret instructions".

The *Tengyur* was codified in 1836 by *Nyima Tenzin* (the 22nd Abbott of Menri Monastery) and contains 131 volumes of commentaries on the four categories of the *Kangyur*. The complete set of volumes includes 131 volumes of *Yungdrung Bön* texts and 169 volumes of New Bön (*Sar ma*) texts, totalling 300 volumes. The *Tengyur* are divided into three categories:

(i) "External", including commentaries on canonical texts dealing with monastic discipline, morality, metaphysics, and the biography of Tonpa Shenrab. (ii) "Internal", comprising the commentaries on the Tantras including rituals focusing on the Tantric' deities and the cult of *Dakinis* (goddesses) whose task it is to protect the doctrine, and worldly rituals of magic and divination. (iii) "Secret", a section that deals with meditational practices.

Change and adherence

Most people tend to be linked with their local shrine and monastery because it is to this centre that they give offerings to the monks and provide practical service. Most of the monks come from the local community and so it is their families who provide for them. At harvest time the young monks go back home to help their families in the fields. In return the monks are called on to chant for the families if there is a death, celebration or misfortune.

In general local families are not aware of which school of Tibetan Buddhism they are associated. I know of one case in which the family watched a television programme on Buddhism in Tibet. This led to a thoughtful discussion as to which school they belonged. They could not easily classify themselves and different members of the family had different views. In general the religious traditions of a family are passed on from one generation to the next, essentially the practices rather than the beliefs.

13 Gompa—the dGelugpa tradition

Gompa is a generic term used for various Tibetan institutions that are in many respects very different. The term here is used for Tibetan religious communities in the eastern area of Tibet. In the Kham and Amdo areas there are medium and large monastic gompas with upwards of 50 to several hundred monks. In the Rgyalrong region about 5-10% of the male population are involved with a monastery and a much smaller percentage of women. Although the numbers are relatively small, their influence is still very significant. This chapter is a study of Caodeng, the largest gompa in the Rgyalrong region located in the extreme north in Ma'erkang County close to the region of Amdo.

Caodeng is a three hour journey by bus from Ma'erkang. The road to the village passes along a narrow valley of one of the feeder rivers to the Dadu River. The steep valley occasionally widens up to allow a small village to be settled surrounded by cultivated fields. Most of the way it is a single track road with only a few passing places as the road slowly makes its way up to the Amdo grasslands. The bus finally halts at the bridge that crosses the river to Caodeng village and monastery. A new concrete road has been constructed by the local authorities which allows easy access to the village about 1 km away.

For the first 200 years of its existence, the monastery was a Bön centre and then at the end of the Ming period it converted to dGelug and has remained such for the last 400 years. The first exponent of the dGelugpa ("yellow hat") tradition known to have entered Rgyalrong was a disciple of Je Tsongkhapa (1357–1419), the famous teacher whose activities led to the formation of the dGelug school in Tibet. The disciple was known as Tsha kho Ngag dbang grangs pa who after completing his studies returned to his homeland in Rgyalrong. Little is known about him except that he is said to have come from the northern *tusi* of Xiaojin.

Tsha kho Ngag dbang grangs pa saw the conversion of a few people to the dGelug school and founded a few small monasteries, but it was not an easy task as the local people were strong adherents of Bön. During the following three centuries dGelug made little inroads. One event that made a significant change was if the local king converted to the new tradition, so that the people of his *tusi* usually followed. One way that this occurred was when the young son of the king's family was recognized as a reincarnation of a dGelug lama. The kings of the northern *tusi* of Zhuokeji, Suomo and Songgong were eventually converted to dGelug sometime in the 1600s. The dGelug however had great difficulty penetrating into southern Rgyalrong as the kings remained staunch adherents of Bön.

The monastery at Caodeng probably converted when the king at Zhuokeji converted. Even though the area is some distance away on the other side of Ma'erkang it came under the control of Zhuokeji. There are remains of an old palace in Caodeng and tradition has it that this was once a strong *tusi* with a palace even larger than that of Zhuokeji. It appears that sometime in the past this palace was taken over by the *tusi* of Zhuokeji and this became his summer palace. In the 1960s the palace was burnt down and little now remains. The dividing line between the *tusis* was a bridge further downstream. The *tusis* were secular rulers whose responsibility was to keep good order and protect the kingdom.

Over the years the monastery of Caodeng has steadily increased in size. Fortunately it was not damaged during the Cultural Revolution and since the beginning of Reform and Opening up, the current leaders have been able to expand and develop the monastery and make it into a place of growing influence. Caodeng is a daughter monastery of the great Kirti Monastery a little further to the north in Aba.

Monastery as a place of residence

In 2010, the monastery had about 500 registered monks and novices, of which 321 stayed permanently in the community. Of this number about 100 are in charge of catering to the needs of different nearby villages while about 200 are resident at the monastery.

There are 200 two-storey buildings that are properly numbered and recorded for the use of the monks. In total about 1,000 monks could be accommodated, but the buildings are often used for storage. This makes Caodeng monastery the largest in the Rgyalrong region even though it is located to the north of the region close to Amdo. The Amdo region is strongly dGelug and Caodeng is located on a major route between Amdo and Rgyalrong. Caodeng has therefore been a major factor for the spread of dGelug into the Rgyalrong valley.

There are no walls surrounding the monastery which the Abbott is quick to explain is for a specific purpose. Buddhism, he would say, is for the people, and so they should have ready access to the halls in the complex. There is however a problem with this view as it allows the cows to easily wander around the complex making a mess. For this reason every three days a person comes to the monastery to collect the dung that is taken to be used for fertilizer.

The courtyard houses are more in Amdo style than Rgyalrong. There may be one to six monks resident in each house. The courtyards make a maze of narrow alleyways with dung covered walls. The oldest buildings date back to the time when the monastery was Bön. The roofs of the major temples are coated with brass which shines like gold in the bright sunshine. Caodeng has the buildings and halls common to dGelug monasteries: (Grand) Sutra Hall, Court of Debating, Stupa Site, Prayer-wheel complex and array, Dharma Protectors Temple, Hall of the Goddess of Mercy, Hall of the Maitreya Buddha, Hall of the Hayagriva plus halls of other gods and deities.

Stupa Hall where the major rituals are performed.

The large distinctive stupa was built in 2010. The white-painted stonework and gold cone make it a major landmark in the valley. A notable element is the Nepali-style, particularly the eyes that are painted facing the four directions. Between each pair of eyes there is a *tilaka* mark common in north India. This design was brought back by pilgrims and migrants who had travelled in Nepal and north India, and wanted to duplicate what they saw. This style of stupa has become increasingly common during the last 20 years showing yet another element of change found in the area.

Monastery as a social organization

Caodeng monastery follows the management structure common to dGelug monasteries throughout China. The Abbott is the most senior person and is recognized as a Living Buddha (Chinese: huófó,

Tibetan: *tulku*), and is usually known by the title of *Rinpoche* meaning the "treasure of human beings". It is considered improper to mention the name of the Abbott directly, so when Tibetans refer to any such sacred monks they would always use the title Rinpoche.

Living Buddhas (*tulku*) are individuals who have been recognized as rebirths of previous lamas or as emanations of deities such as Avalokitesvara and Manjusri. This provides a means by which the succession to monastic leadership (the so-called "thrones") is regulated especially among the dGelugpa as the monks and abbots are supposed to be celibate. It also enables certain aristocratic families with significant estates to maintain their hold on monasteries (Mills, 2000). New *tulku* are recognized through certain tests and prophecies that come under the responsibility of a special committee to identify Living Buddhas. This organization now consists of both government officials and monks who work together to identify the reincarnate Living Buddhas. The Chinese authorities are aware of the importance of the *tulku* and many are granted special opportunities for education in Chengdu or Beijing. Some even become important government cadres, but this can sometimes be a delicate position during times of local unrest.

The Rinpoche chairs the Monastic Management Committee (called the *Congdem*). This includes three persons with the titles *Wembo*, *Ghegu* and *Kanbo*, and together with the Abbott they carry out all matters related to belief, politics and economy of the monastery. The committee is often said to be elected, but it is unclear who is eligible to vote. Most Abbotts are in one way or another associated with the CCP, and are careful to follow the given guidelines. For their good services they are usually provided by the Party with an apartment in a designated area of Chengdu.

The *Wembo* is the general manager of the monastery and can act as the chair of the board in the absence of the Abbot. The role is also called *Ghentsam* in some monasteries, and he has the absolute power to decide about most practical things in the monastery.

The title *Ghegu* means "the master in the hall", and he is responsible for discipline in the monastery. His role is particularly significant during communal chanting and debates. He ensures that nobody falls asleep or becomes distracted by other things. He is generally feared by the younger monks as he carries with him an iron rod which he is not slow to use. This position usually rotates annually, but the person is chosen directly by the Abbott.

The *Kanbo* is one of two *Ghepa* and he is in charge of finances. The practical aspects of the monastery such as merchandise, shops, restaurants and warehouses all come under the auspices of his assistant called *Gee Wha*. His responsibility is to acquire money for the Abbott and the monastery as a whole. Because of his practical role, his favour is often sought by monks.

In addition to this monastic committee there is also a Chinese Communist Party (CCP) committee. These are common in all larger monasteries in western China. This committee does cause some constraints for the monastery, but in the presence of visitors monks generally focus on the benefits of having such a committee. For example, in Caodeng money has recently been given for the building of a concrete-surfaced road to connect the monastery to the main road. The village has its own primary school and police station. There are also a few members of the police resident in the monastery dressed as monks, but their identity is usually known to most of the monks. Their duty is to monitor activities going on in the monastery and report any new visitors especially if they are foreigners.

Larger monasteries are often organized into residential houses called *khang tsen*. These cluster around monks from a particular region, and provide residential and social support. Some groups become something like an internal police force that imposes the rule of the *Ghegu*. These monks are called *Dapdop* who can sometimes act more like a gang of thugs and are disliked especially by the younger monks. Goldstein in his book called them "punk-monks" because of their rough manner and gang violence (Goldstein, 1997). Their behaviour sometimes goes beyond acceptable limits, but their power is such that expulsion is rarely possible. During the big festivals they are responsible for maintaining public order.

Big monasteries, whether Buddhist or Bön, have *Zhacang*, which are similar to the colleges or departments within universities. They come under the *Congdem*. The name of *Zhacang* is derived from *Zhapa*, the Tibetan name for junior monk. The four most common *Zhacang*s are *Deyang*, *Gomang*, *Ngapa* and *Losehling*, which are all managed by the *Kanbo* or Abbott. These departments usually relate to *tshannyid* (philosophy), *Juepa* (Tantrism), *Ten Kor* (Astrology) and *Mangpa* (medicine). Older monks usually specialize in one or other of these disciplines.

Tibetan medicine is one of the disciplines found in the larger monasteries. The hospital at Caodeng monastery was expanded in 2009-10 so as to be able to accommodate a greater number of patients. By 2012 it also had a medical school with a teacher named Tintsen Rinpoche and 20 regular students. Treatment is usually through the prescription of the herbs that are found on the grasslands around the monastery.

Monastery as a place of ritual

The dGelug tradition has made the ethical and monastic discipline of the *Vinaya* a central part of its spiritual practice. The Vinaya comes from the early Theravada tradition and was originally compiled in the Pali language. The dGelug is the only school of Vajrayana Buddhism that prescribes monastic ordination as a necessary qualification and basis for its teachers (lamas). Lay people are usually not permitted to give initiations if there are teachers with monastic vows within close proximity. This discipline was laid down by Tsongkhapa as a way of preventing Buddhist teachings from further degenerating. Je Rinpoche later showed how Vajrayana teachings could be practiced without compromising Vinaya with its teaching about outward calm and controlled demeanour. In Tibet this is based upon the internal poise associated with the two stages of the yogic practitioner. Tsongkhapa's explanation adopts both sutra and tantra as mutually complementary paths.

Each year an examination is held for those who have completed their studies. In it their performance is evaluated by the abbot of the particular college. The topics for their dialectical examination are drawn from the whole course of study and the topic to be debated is selected by the abbot on the spot, so that students have no chance to do specific preparation. Thus it is a real test of a student's abilities and the depth of his understanding. At the conclusion the abbot assigns each candidate to a category of *Geshe* according to his ability. There are four such categories, *Dorampa*, *Lingtse*, *Tsorampa* and *Lharampa—Lharampa* being the highest. After this, in order to qualify, the *Geshe* candidates are not allowed to miss even one of the three daily debate sessions during the subsequent eight months. One of the key figures in the debates is the *Ghegu* mentioned earlier, who is the monk in charge of discipline who carries the iron rod.

Further examination of the organization shows that Tibetan monastic institutions are part of a vast network of "mother-daughter" monasteries that continue to expand (Miller, 1961). There are about a dozen "mother" monasteries, each of which has many subsidiary monasteries scattered throughout the whole of the Tibetan area, and sometimes beyond. Major subsidiary monasteries like Caodeng have their own daughter monasteries in the region. The mother monastery is the training ground for the heads of its various subsidiaries. Even in the most remote areas, ascending the ladder of ecclesiastic rank is dependent upon training at one of the mother centres. Not even incarnate lamas can assume controlling positions until they have received such instruction. The mother monastery maintains ties with its "daughters" in various other ways, such as in the form of economic aid. This is often through the periodic visitations of high-ranking monks who assume leadership of the local monastery during their stay. In many instances, suggestions and advice from the mother monastery form part of the normal business of the local monastery's biweekly convocations.

For outsiders, there are always those things that leave one puzzled together with the realisation that more is going on than you are aware. For example in May 2013 the senior Abbott at Caodeng unexpectedly died just before a major festival. Instead of his body being disposed of in the most prestigious way it was decided that it was to be quickly cremated. It is true that there were few vultures around at that time of the year, but there was certainly an element of mystery here from which many were excluded.

Monks also act like priests providing ritual services for laypeople who in turn support them. This must not be confused with another monastic task which is that of allowing laypeople to gain merit. Although, the Vinaya forbids monks and nuns from engaging in practices such as astrology, medicine or ritual performance, over the centuries these practices have flourished. In Tibetan Buddhism the great majority of monks adopt a priestly function (Dreyfus, 2003).

This may sound surprising to those who think of monasteries as places of rational philosophy and meditation. Most local monasteries tend to be devoted to meeting the ritual needs of the laity of the area, and hence their schedule revolves around ritual. Even in the large monasteries, rituals take precedence over everything else. It is because the monasteries so emphasize ritual that those monks who want to focus on meditation leave the monastery to go to some isolated hermitage.

The rituals are performed in the assembly hall at the centre of the monastery, where all the monks gather. This activity therefore symbolizes the monastery as a community. Each monastery is very proud of the assembly hall, into which it invests much time, effort and money. A large assembly hall signifies the strength of the monastery as demonstrated in the number of monks taking part in the rituals. The assembly hall is the centre for the distribution of monastic income—there sponsors give the monks tea, food and money.

An important category of monastic rituals are those prescribed by the Vinaya. The first of these is the confession held every fortnight. Here monks confess any failure in fulfilling the 227 rules of the monk set out in the Vinaya.

A second group of rituals relate to annual events such as the ritual marking the beginning and closing of the rainy season retreat. An important event is the celebration of the Buddha's birth, enlightenment and passing away, which usually occurs in May. Monasteries often celebrate the passing away of their founder. For example, dGelugpa commemorate Dzong-ka-ba's passing away, and Nyingma Padmadambhava's passing.

In Caodeng an important festival takes place after the Tibetan New Year of *Losar*, usually in March. This lasts for four weeks and every day hundreds of monks join to chant. The number of monks can be as many as 2,000, but it is never less than 500. Monks are continually coming and going during the festival as their other commitments allow. Each monastery has its own individual traditions revolving around a particular deity who is worshipped during these elaborate ceremonies which can last several days.

Another important festival occurs in Caodeng usually in May. It commences with the "Grand Auspicious Prayer", and aims to bring blessing upon every region of the local biosphere. At the beginning of the period the surrounding land is brown and barren, but by the end colour is coming to the landscape as new shoots emerge. In 2013 some 300 monks and 700 laypeople attended, and the rituals continued day and night for 7 days. During this time the participants repeated the great mantra *Oṃ mani padme hum* 200 million times. This is not a common dGelugpa festival, and actually has more associations with Bönpa. The lay people tend to see the ritual as the spiritual force bringing about the spring growth. This can also be a time when epidemics are common, and so it is considered to be an auspicious activity to prevent disease.

A third set of rituals are those specific to a particular monastery. Each monastery has its own daily ritual cycle, which may include rituals performed by the majority of the resident monks every day. Protectors of the monastery are briefly propitiated. There is often an evening debate in the dGelug monasteries involving a long ritual that includes repeated praises to Tara and recitation of the Heart Sutra.

Another very common category of rituals is that called "foot firming" (*zhabs brtan*) which have various instrumental purposes. This may be to cure disease, repel evil spirits or bring luck in various activities etc. Foot-firming rituals are performed at the request of those who are ill or are facing hardship. These could be requested by the laity, monks or by corporate entities such as the authorities in the Tibetan area. Their timing is determined either by consultation of an astrological calendar or divination performed by a monk. If they are to be performed by the entire monastery, all the monks gather in the assembly hall. In return, they at least receive tea from the sponsors and sometimes food and money. These rituals may alternatively be performed by a few monks in the sponsor's home. These rituals build a network of supporters who come to rely on the monastery in times of crises and are therefore willing to be quite generous. They are an important source of income to the monastery as a whole.

Individual monks may spend much time on these rituals, which help to provide some of their support. Although some monks find these a distraction to scholarly pursuits, many love these occasions because they enable them to eat better food, make some money and find additional sponsors. They also enjoy the complexity of the performance and chants.

The practice of rituals in Tibetan monastic life illustrates the complex interactions of the layers of Tibetan religious culture. First are those belonging to the Vinaya rituals of the Theravada (Hinayana) tradition. Second, some belong to the exoteric Mahayana tradition. Third, and most common, are those rituals that are tantric in origin having been domesticated and transformed into monastic rituals. Sometimes the exoteric and esoteric aspects are mixed while on other occasions they are kept distinct.

Monastery as a place of education

Traditionally the monastery has been the focus of education within the Tibetan region. The model of education is however quite different from that common in the West. It is in fact more akin to Scholasticism of Europe and Islam in the later Middle Ages (1000-1500). One of the most fascinating discussions of the educational model of a Tibetan monastery is that given by Dreyfus who is one of the few westerners who has qualified as a Geshe (Dreyfus, 2003).

The first element of education is memorization. The master in charge of the scholar would choose a book written by a renowned scholar as a subject for investigation. By reading it thoroughly and critically, the disciple is expected to learn and appreciate the theories of the author. Other documents related to the book would be referenced, and the points of disagreement would be noted. In the West, we tend to seek to understand first and then memorize a passage. In the Tibetan tradition it is often only through the process of memorizing the text that the student gains insight into the inner meaning. Westerners usually find memorization of vast amounts of texts difficult, but to memorize texts one doesn't understand is even more of a challenge.

A second element in learning is through debating which is a dialectic process. In Scholasticism, once the sources and points of disagreement had been laid out in a series of dialectics, the two sides of an argument would be made whole so that they would be found to be in agreement and not contradictory. This was done in two ways. The first was through philological analysis in which words are examined and their multiple meanings dissected. The issue is also explored as to whether the author might have intended a certain word to mean something different than the general meaning. Ambiguity therefore is used to find common ground between two otherwise contradictory statements. The second way is through logical analysis, which relies on the rules of formal logic to show that contradictions did not exist but are subjective to the reader.

Debate taking place in Gelugpa monastery.

In Tibetan monastic education this process is achieved through the well-known process of debate. Starting from common opinions, the debaters will proceed to various deductions. By debate they will adopt the most likely conclusion. The process is essentially a game, which requires both competition and honest participation. However, there are various lawful tricks such as playing on words, using false premises and limiting time for reply. It should be noted that only a small percent of those who choose the monastic way of life seek the path to become a Geshe.

Relationship between sacred and secular

In practical terms the monastery serves as a centre of education and the cultivation of the arts even though only a small percentage of the monks participate in these. The monastery does this by absorbing surplus labour when the population is more than that required for economic purposes. It is a socially valued alternative to the life of herding and farming. Many of the young monks come from local villages and grasslands that support the monastery. The monks are required to help the families during harvest or other times when extra labour is required. Local families can also be critical of the monastery if it grows too large and places an excessive load upon them. I have heard comments such as, "We don't need a monastery so large. Half the number of monks would be adequate for the rituals."

For religious girls and women nunneries exist, but the numbers are much smaller than those for men. One reason for this is that nuns continue to live with their families more often than do monks, and so continue to contribute to household tasks while pursuing their religious activities. Another reason is that donations generally favour the monks and the monasteries rather than the nuns, and so nuns in nunneries can often face economic hardship.

Most monks enter the monastery as children, which used to be the main source of education in the Tibetan region. Basic literacy in the Tibetan language was common among monks and nuns, though fewer were inclined to pursue advanced studies. Today, 9-years free education is available and compulsory throughout China, so most children attend one of the primary or middle schools in the towns.

The few studies that have been made on the life of young Tibetan monks come from Nepal as shown in the video *Tsundu: Becoming a Lama* (Raji Mani Gurung, 1997). This describes the life of one young novice who arises at 5.30 am for early morning *pujas* and is portrayed as following the daily discipline of chanting, study and meals. As Brian Given (Given, 1997) comments in his review of the film, little is actually said about the social life of the young monks and the strong bonds that develop between those who live in the same household.

When I have asked the young monks in Sichuan about their life, they are quick to respond that they do not find it boring. Food for the monks is cooked in a large metal wok. The limited choice is between porridge or milk tea, which for the young monks is a continual source of complaint. They then attend the chanting in the temple that occurs most days, and perform routine duties for their household. In their free time they meet with their peers to play cards, watch television and drink tea. They often go to the nearby village to play pool or sit in the teashops to gossip and make rude comments about any passing visitors.

Larger monasteries have a shop to provide the items that monks may need. Here can be bought robes, beads, silk scarves, offering bowls as well as practical things like soap and toothpaste, cups and plates, as well as washing bowls and cloth.

Young monks like young men everywhere are interested to meet young women. The "secular" village next to the monastery provides a suitable opportunity. The girls generally like the young monks because they are considered to be cleaner than the nomads who smell of yaks and smoke.

New Developments

The Management Team is not only concerned about developing the monastery, but would like to make the village a model for others to emulate. They have people whose task is to raise funds for the monastery and new developments.

Throughout China monasteries and temples are seeing considerable redevelopment. The more attractive and convenient the complex, the more people it attracts. Today wealthy tourists from the city with a religious inclination are frequently journeying to different monasteries. Monasteries are therefore eager to provide beautiful temple buildings as well as accommodation and services for the new visitors. The line between religious tourism and pilgrimage is rather indistinct.

At Caodeng a new entrance gate with a walkway up to the main temple has been completed to make a grand entrance that adds prestige to the monastery as a whole. However, an issue has arisen with the walkway that illustrates some of the tensions that can occur in a monastic complex. Although the walkway has been widened, one house owner refuses to reduce the size of his garden, which sticks out spoiling the lines of the entrance. It is certain that the man will eventually relent, but he is wanting to express his disapproval and, if possible get some recompense.

This illustrates that many of the local people are not happy with the increasing demands that the monastery is putting on them. During the building season, which is usually October-November before the snows come, many people are required to give their labour for free for the new buildings. This, of course, takes them away from their own projects. In addition, some skilled craftsmen claimed not to have been paid for two years.

Challenges have emerged in that although previously the village was built on flat land, the houses were built close together to conserve as much land as possible for agriculture. The *tusi* encouraged this as it also enables him to keep control. Today people want more space around their houses, which means there is less farmland. The construction of the new monastery building is requiring much new timber, which goes against the intention of conserving the local environment.

Another new venture is a nursing home for local aged people. By 2013 this had grown to 75 residents, and was certainly meeting a need in the community.

Plans are also underway for the construction of a local museum after the style of the cultural centres started in the Badi area. At Caodeng the aim is to develop centres focussing on three aspects: religion, crafts and intangible heritage. It is not surprising that at Caodeng it has been the religious aspect that has progressed most rapidly with the construction of a residence ("palace") for the head of Kirti monastery who is currently in exile in India.

In November 2013 a major festival of the whole of the Kirti monastery network occurred in Caodeng as part of the 60th celebrations for the liberation of Aba Autonomous Region. This celebration should occur every year, but since liberation it has only occurred three times, once at Kirti monastery, once at Charli monastery and then at Caodeng. With the series of self-immolations that have been occurring this became a politically sensitive event. It was not only politically sensitive, but also presented many ceremonial challenges to accommodate the expected 3,000 monks. The main hall can accommodate only a few hundred for the ceremonies, so the courtyard in front of the temple has been extended to seat 2,000. This area was carpeted, and 3,000 cushions provided for those attending. This required a massive financial outlay for the monastery which was eager to put on the best show.

Many of the monks were housed with local families. Five to twenty monks were placed with each family, depending on the wealth of the family. Catering during the day was provided in the monastery. The highest 300 monks were catered for in new dining faculties built in the west of the monastery. The remainder were catered in the existing faculties in the east.

* * * *

These three chapters have discussed the variety of religious practices found among the Rgyalrongwa. The gompas provide a social and religious network that stretches across the Tibetan world of which the Dalai Lama is the supreme head. In practice most ordinary people associate themselves with their local monastery, supporting their family members who are resident monks. As one moves away from this vast network, the rituals become more like that which has been called "folk" religion or even superstition. This Tibetan religious world view is however being challenged by the secular forces of change, and perhaps most specifically for the minority people of China, by the growth of tourism and secular education.

14 Tourism

After discussing some of the specific aspects of change in Rgyalrong society it is necessary to look at two major influences that have impacted the society in many ways—tourism and secular education. Both of these have been encouraged by central government and as a result, have been accepted by local people.

Tourism is big business in China, and has been developed to help rural populations combat poverty, especially among Tibetans and other ethnic minorities. In 1999, Sichuan province announced that it had initiated a dozen new tour routes as part of the 1999 nationwide *Eco-Tourism Campaign*. The list included tours that connected the ancient pilgrimage sites of Emei Shan and Leshan located to the south of Chengdu, with the famous Jiuzhaigou and Huanglong Nature Reserves in the Tibetan areas to the north. In addition, river rafting, hiking along ancient mountain paths, and trips to areas rich in flora and fauna were planned (Schrempf & Hayes, 2009). Then in 2001 the State Council resolution *On Further Accelerating the Development of the Tourism Sector* called for the establishment of "experimental zones for poverty alleviation through tourism" as well as the construction of new airports and roads.

Various studies have been made of the impact of tourism in western China. Tim Oakes studied the region of Guizhou and Ashild Kolas looked at tourism in Yunnan Provinces (Kolas, 2005; Oakes, 1998). Both highlighted the importance and power of the state in producing political and economic outcomes in ethnic tourism. Oakes emphasized how the mechanisms to develop tourist areas in Guizhou helped to both "civilize" the local people, and respond to official calls for correct notions and practices. Kolas discussed similar issues in the construction of the imaginary land of 'Shangrila' in northern Yunnan. Later Schrempf and Hayes in their study of the town of Songpan, which is just east of the main Rgyalrong area showed the so-called "commoditization" of culture. Underlying all these papers is the question as to who actually benefits from tourism (Schrempf & Hayes, 2009).

The Dadu valley opened to tourism in 1999 when the local authorities considered this to be a suitable way of developing the region and discouraging the people from illegal logging. From this time many Han Chinese and some overseas tourists have ventured into the beautiful valley especially during the national holidays—the so-called "golden weeks" (usually the weeks at the beginning of May and October). As with tourism in other areas, this has raised challenges in seeking to meet the demands of the visitors and the expectations of the hosts.

New hotels have been built in the towns of Ma'erkang and Danba and a motel has been constructed on the main tourist route from Danba north to Ma'erkang. The motel lies close to the road alongside the river and provides useful overnight accommodation for those who have driven into the region. The design of the accommodation, food and evening dances match the general picture that most Han visitors have of Tibetan life. A more extensive project has been the construction of a new model village.

A Model Village

Danba Jiaju Tibetan Village is located just a few kilometres north of Danba, and was built by the local authorities as a representation of a Rgyalrong village in a beautiful valley. Tourist websites write of it as "Tibetan Fairyland ….. Jiaju Tibetan Village is a great destination for photography. It is one of the most beautiful *ancient* villages, voted for by the Chinese National Geographic in 2005" (emphasis mine). More recently it has been of research interest to Chinese anthropologists in studying Ethnic Tourism (Dai Min, 2010).

The houses in the village were built by the authorities and are owned by them until the local residents have fully paid for their new property. In practice, most of the residents continue to live in their traditional houses a short distant from Jiaju village as this allows them to keep their animals, and remain near their family and friends. Visitors to the valley are charged a small fee to enter and visit the houses. Part of this income is taken by the authorities and the majority is divided equally amongst the villagers. Families who host the guests are paid directly.

In looking at the houses in the model village, two major modifications have been made to the design, which are aimed at providing greater convenience for the tourists. First, there are no animals in the village. One of the common comments of tourists in entering a traditional Rgyalrong house is the smell of the animals. Personally I have never found this particularly offensive, but the presence of farm animals on the ground under the living rooms causes tourists some amusement and disgust.

A second modification is that the house owners have been encouraged to decorate their houses in a much more elaborate style than was usual for them which they call "Lhasa style". This was further encouraged by the presence of an artist from Dege (in the far west of Sichuan next to the Tibetan Autonomous Region) who was resident in the area. He decorated the rooms of the houses in an ornate style with the eight auspicious symbols: conch, umbrella, banner, fish, dharma wheel, endless knot, lotus and vase. In addition there are often figures of mountain lions in the mystic scenes of the heavens. Tourists consider this style as being more authentic, and they certainly make the rooms more photogenic. (See following photograph of a guesthouse in Suopo).

A guesthouse in Suopo that has been decorated
in "Lhasa style" to attract tourists

The attitude of the tourists has had an effect on the local people that John Urry has called the "tourist gaze" (Urry, 1990). The people have become aware of their own distinctive culture and that visitors consider this to be not only different, but in some ways primitive. This is illustrated in the way tourists often reacted to the smell of the animals for which the local people are usually both embarrassed and apologetic.

The village has been built to meet the tourist quest for an experience of an "authentic" Tibetan village, but with mod-cons. The local people have therefore worked with the local authorities to construct an alternative lifestyle that MacCannell has called "staged authenticity" (MacCannell, 1973). Whilst tourists speak of the village as being "authentic", other people in the region see Jiaju distinctly as a tourist village different from other Rgyalrong villages.

Local initiative

Nevertheless the relative success of the Jiaju village has encouraged families in other villages to take some initiative and offer to host tourists. Easy access to the main road is a major requirement as tourists come by car and are not willing to travel far up difficult winding tracks. One such place that has become popular with tourists is Suopo located a little south of Danba. It has the advantage of being easily visible from the main road that runs along the west side of the valley. The numerous stone towers on the hillside make the view across the river a great photo opportunity such that in 2010 a car park and viewing platform were constructed by the authorities. More adventurous visitors cross the river by the iron bridge and make their way up to the village.

In Suopo several of the villagers have extended their homes, and some have even constructed purpose built houses to accommodate tourists. As in Jiaju they have decorated the guest rooms in the "Lhasa-style" to make them appear more authentic. The local people know full well what they have done and for what reason—to make money. The ceilings of the guest houses have been ornately painted as have the walls and beds. There are no animals close to the house, and a solar water heater located on the roof provides hot water for the visitors to shower. Electricity is available in each room not only for light, but to allow tourists to charge their cell phones, tablets and camera batteries. For some of the older people who have never left the valley this has brought them into direct contact not only with the tourists, but also with the technology of the modern world.

The hosts not only provide accommodation for the tourists, but also a variety of home cooked local foods. For a small sum the visitor can dress in traditional costume and have their photographs taken. There is usually a range of local handicrafts for sale. Houses built close to one of the towers have turned their location into an advantage. Flags are attached to the tower visually indicating that the tower can be climbed and is open to visitors for a small charge. Many of the tourists are eager to climb the ladders in the tower in order to view the scenery. During the "golden weeks" many tourists come to the region, and the hosts are happy to accommodate and feed many. This brings them considerable extra income in addition to that made from farming.

The specific location of the house has had an effect on the success of such ventures. Houses closest to the main road are those to which tourists immediately go as are those houses next to a tower. As a result families living further up the hillside distant from the main road receive few or no visitors, which means those families living closer to the road are getting additional income from tourism while those further away receive little. A wealth gap has therefore begun to grow among the villagers, which produces tensions among families. It is notable that since 2011 a charge has been made for tourists coming into the village of Suopo which is shared amongst all the villagers in the same way as in Jiaju. This partly helps to share the benefits of tourism amongst all the villagers, but some tension still exists.

To control the development of private initiatives in hosting tourists, the government has implemented a scheme to give qualifying accommodation the status of authorized tourist accommodation. Those who have been so acknowledged proudly display the government plaque on the entrance to their houses.

Meeting the tourist quest

In an attempt to meet the needs and interests of tourists the local people have implemented other changes. In addition to the elaboration of the guesthouses villagers have sought to develop local areas of interest. This could be by improving a local stupa or temple to make it more attractive to visitors. One example can be seen in the village of Badi located in the main valley. The main north-south road runs through the village near where it crosses a tributary of the Dadu River next to a small bridge. For many years there has been a stupa in this place as is common at most places in Tibet where rivers join or there are places of danger. Stupas provide spiritual protection at the junction. Here the local people have constructed a new more elaborate stupa that readily attracts the attention of tourists driving along the road. Tourists now stop their cars and get out in order to take photographs. On entering the walled area around the stupa, arrows point to the anticlockwise direction visitors should take as they walk around the Bön stupa. There is something of a mutual competition between villages to attract the few tourists that come to the region.

A development that has been encouraged by the research team has been the building of what was called "cultural centres". In earlier times each village would have a dance area where members of the village would congregate to talk, sing and dance. With the changes that have come to the region, these spaces have been lost. The suggestion was made that the university team would provide cement for the floor of the dance area if the villagers would do the building. This was eagerly accepted and in a number of villages walled dance areas have been constructed. In addition, cooking facilities have been built to provide food for festivals and weddings. Amplifiers were acquired to provide the music that would echo across the valley. These areas have proved very popular as they allow the villagers once more to congregate and enjoy time together.

In addition it was proposed was that these "cultural centres" could also be centres to display the traditional culture of the people. The aim was to initiate museums designed by local people themselves rather than foreign experts along the lines described by Joy Hendry. (Hendry, 2005:38-47). Here, it was hoped the villagers could exhibit some of their local skills and artefacts. The suggestion was that the people themselves should select and arrange the items rather than this being done by some foreign expert. In this way the local people would be able to express something of their own heritage to tourists.

This aspect of the suggestion has proved less successful. Although old tools, furniture or other items were being discarded, the people saw little reason for storing even the best of these. Whereas the team thought that this would be a way in which they could tell their story, the people were more practical and wondered who would want to see their old rubbish. What they wanted was to make the centre not a museum, but a living place—a social centre. Apart from cooking facilities, they have built a concrete table for the young people to play table tennis. This is a place people can come to talk, have fun and discuss issues of common concern. The team was pleasantly surprised that the residents of several other villages asked for help in buying the cement so that they too could build a cultural centre. Whereas the villagers were previously somewhat fragmented they now had a centre for the social life of the village.

As in most tourist areas souvenirs have become a commodity item for sale to the visitors. As was mentioned in chapter 6 the team deliberately sought to encourage this in the locality through revitalizing some of the indigenous skills: black pottery, needlework, baskets. None of these were particularly successful from a financial point of view as explained in an earlier chapter.

In recent years fewer tourists have come to the region. The earthquake of 2008 destroyed some of the infrastructure, and the construction of the hydroelectric schemes has spoilt what were previously designated on maps as "sightseeing spots". Nevertheless, tourists do come at major holiday periods and this provides an additional boost to the local economy, but for much of the year hotels and guesthouses have only a few visitors.

15 Education

In addition to tourism an even greater factor that has affected the local culture has been modern education. It was not until 1934 that the first schools were set up in the Tibetan area, but these had only a few students. With the founding of the People's Republic of China public education was especially encouraged in the minority areas with the purpose of "civilizing" the people who inhabited the frontiers of China. As Catriona Bass writes:

> The Chinese Communist project of the last five decades has essentially been presented as a moral project, one of remoulding the cultures of its nationalities into a unitary modern socialist culture, based on Han Chinese culture (Catriona Bass, 2005).

During the 1950s, schools were set up throughout the Tibetan areas, and from 1952 some young Tibetans were sent away to colleges in major cities such as the Nationalities Institutes in Beijing and Chengdu. Many Tibetans welcomed these educational opportunities and even some *Geshe* monks sought employment in the Nationalities Institutes. During the period 1956-58 a number of primary schools were set up as bilingual schools (*shuangyu*—a combination of Tibetan and Chinese), but following the Lhasa Uprising of 1959 and the widespread famine of 1962 these were closed. Then during the Cultural Revolution of 1967-76 education in minority areas was abolished altogether. Communes were told to establish their own schools, but these were only in Chinese.

Bilingual education and Tibetan-language instruction disappeared for a period of about 20 years until about 1978 when the education of minorities was once again promoted by Central Government (Catriona Bass, 1998).

A significant step at this time was the introduction of a minorities version of the College Entrance Examination (*minzu gaokao,* or for short *minkao*) in the late 1970s. It initially differed from the regular *gaokao* only by the addition of Tibetan as an examination subject, but students had to choose between using Tibetan or Chinese language for each of the *minkao* subjects. Most students, however, chose to use Chinese language in their exams for all subjects except Tibetan language itself. This was because all the textbooks were in Chinese and the students had done all their homework in Chinese. As students were not allowed to mix languages within a *minkao* subject most students chose Chinese.

In 1984 autonomous areas were given the right to train and employ cadres belonging to the ethnic minorities, develop education and ethnic culture as well as speak and write in the local language. This was promoted under the slogan "Putting more Tibetans in the Saddle". Most of the autonomous areas then began to set up their own local educational programmes resulting in the expansion of the teaching of Tibetan.

In 1987, the Tibetan Autonomous Region (TAR) Congress passed a resolution stipulating that all junior middle schools were to use Tibetan as the medium of instruction by 1993. This year was designated as the "Year of Education in the TAR" which resulted in more money being made available for education. By 1994 educational expenditure had doubled that of the 1990 level (1995 TAR Statistical Yearbook). However, riots in Lhasa focused mainly on Han Chinese businesses, which once more resulted in a crackdown. Bilingual education lost favour in TAR.

In 1994, the policy of sending Tibetan children to study at the minorities universities in Beijing or Chengdu was extended to include Han Chinese students living in the Tibetan region. This further decreased the number of students studying Tibetan in secondary and higher education. Then, in July 1997 Chen Kuiyuan (the TAR Party

Secretary) made a speech in which he advocated a return to the orthodox Marxist view of culture. A concept of a separate Tibetan culture was condemned as "obscuring the dividing line between classes". Quoting Chairman Mao, Chen went on to say that "in inheriting culture, it is necessary to analyse it, to discard its dross, and carry forward the good parts" (Chen, 1997). The Chinese government also instigated an "Anti-Dalai Lama" campaign, with the outcome that Tibetan language instruction at the secondary level was abandoned in TAR.

Outside TAR, the policy changes have not always followed those of TAR and each province has adopted its own policy. As a result there are large variations even among counties, which make the situations difficult to analyse. One common feature is to have two parallel classes in schools for Tibetans: one taught in Chinese and the other in Tibetan. This two track system has enabled students to continue their education in Tibetan from primary to university level. In the Provinces of Gansu and Sichuan senior middle-school graduates have various options such as the South-West Nationalities Institute (*Xinan Minzu Xueyuan*) or a vocational college that could lead to a degree course in a major university.

The 1995-2000 National Project of Compulsory Education in Impoverished Areas programme allocated billions of yuan to improve school conditions in poor areas. In the Ministry of Education programme covering this five year period, the government introduced measures to realize the aim of implementing nine-years of compulsory education in China's western region and eliminate illiteracy among young people and the middle-aged. At the same time, the government promoted the development of modern distance learning for rural elementary and high schools, and further improved rural education management systems.

Nevertheless, the examination system is still based on a nationalized curriculum that is standardized for all subjects at all levels. As Upton writes, "despite wide variation in geography, agriculture, climate, language and local customs, the same subjects are taught with the same materials almost all over the country" (Upton, 1999: 219). The underlying theme in the standardized curriculum projects is the message that "China is a unified, glorious country with a great past, an uncertain but improving present and a bright future" (Upton, 1999: 219). To promote this sense of national unity the nationalized curriculum policy downplays the culture and identity of ethnic minorities.

The common practice is for minority students to receive "bonus points" when they take exams in Chinese. However, the extra points do little to make up for the deficits of taking an examination in a foreign or second language. This preferential policy would seem to make higher education more accessible to minorities but minorities, especially Tibetans, are still under-represented at the university level. Many scholars have concluded that the "bonus points system" is a failure and that it continues to prevent minority students from fully participating in the Chinese educational system (Johnson, Bönnie, 2002: 144).

Universal primary education was implemented by Sichuan Province and Ganzi Prefecture in 1992 and student enrolment continues to be more than 99%. However, the dropout rate is still high with an average of about 8% in recent years. According to statistics for one area, the first grade enrolment was about 440 students in 2003. In 2009, the actual number of school graduates was only 402 students. The rate of attrition of students is slightly higher than the annual average.

The story of one young lady illustrates the context of student attrition. She dropped out of school after 5 years' study, and stayed at home to look after her younger siblings and work on the farm. When she was 13 years old, she left the area to go and work as a waitress and singer with another girl from her home village who had already worked outside for 3 years. By the time she was interviewed she had already worked in Jiuzhaigou, Chengdu, Beijing and Shanghai. When asked the reason why she did not to go back to school she answered:

> They all think I am stupid and I did not learn well, besides other people looked down upon me. In that case, I might as well go out with older sisters to earn money. My parents say that our living place was so poor that no one can go to university from there. Even if you stay at school for more years and you work hard,

you will still only herd sheep after school. A person who does not read any books herds sheep better than those who study for many years. What advantage is it that they can write their names? It is nothing. Now we only need to learn Chinese writing and counting so that when we go out to work we can know if we are being cheated.

This young woman illustrates the views of many of the younger generation in Rgyalrong who are dismissing education as a possible stepping stone to life in the cities. They feel disadvantaged because they do not have the money or the academic ability to succeed in the examinations. For many, manual labour, work in restaurants and entertainment provide a more practical option to make money.

Schools in the Rgyalrong area

Throughout the Rgyalrong region many of the larger villages have primary schools. These are known as *wan xiao* (primary schools with 1-6 grades) and *cun xiao* (village primary schools with only 1-4 grades or less). Village primary schools are built according to the common pattern that is found throughout China. A wall encloses a playground in which are constructed the teaching and dining room blocks. The buildings are 3 or 4 storeys in height, with a stairway in the centre of the building that leads to classrooms on the right and left at each floor. Teacher's rooms and offices are on the ground floor.

Many children have to walk several miles to the school, and often they can be seen winding their way down the mountain paths. The school day begins with the raising of the Chinese national flag and singing of the national anthem. The primary curriculum in the small village schools consists of courses in Ideology and Morality, Tibetan language and Mathematics. The larger urban primary schools have additional courses in Chinese, English, Art, Sport and Social Science.

In practice, therefore, rural children studying in the Tibetan language receive a greater percentage of exposure to Moral Education, which lead Li Maosen to write:

> Moral education in China is basically the expressed thoughts of political leaders, which intrude into other branches of education. As such, it is a means of political indoctrination. Unchanging in purpose, it varies in degree and content as political leaders and policies change. (Li, 1990).

Middle schools are located in the larger villages and towns such as Ma'erkang and Danba and these provide accommodation for students living further away. These students travel home for weekends if their families can afford the transport costs.

Typical Middle school in the Rgyalrong area.

In recent years the number of children in the smaller more isolated villages has declined due to parents going to work in Chengdu, Kangding or a more distant city. Although children are often left at home to be looked after by grandparents many are now moving with their parents to the cities. The result is that many of the village schools are unviable and are being closed. This means that even primary school students have to live at the schools in the towns and come home only at weekends and school holidays. As one Tibetan scholar comments:

> Because they are subjected for long-periods to Han district education, their values change.... Tibetan speaking comrades look down on their school-fellows maintaining that people who learn only the Han language but do not understand their own language and, even less their own culture, are useless (Baden, 1997:15).

Schools and change

Schools are the representatives of modern culture and these interact with villages who are the representatives of Tibetan culture. Many questions are raised through this interaction. Perhaps the most important question as far as this book is concerned is: How do schools become a place in which both modern civilization and traditional heritage can be passed on to the younger generation? Thinking of ways to solve this problem would be a key to the effective functioning of rural schools.

The main task of school teachers is to enable students to further their education along the same lines as those in city schools. In minority areas, this causes the schools to be culturally isolated from the local communities. Government schools therefore find it difficult to play any meaningful part in passing on the cultural heritage. Many teachers commented to me about the importance of the traditional culture, which they considered should be part of school education to ensure the survival of the villages. Both villagers and teachers are interested in combining cultural resources with that of school education, but as yet there are few effective ways of doing this. How might this be done?

Generally teachers have a strong desire to be carriers of the local cultural heritage, and many actively carry out various extra-curricular educational activities together with the villagers. Often they will join with the children in the evenings to take part in some of the traditional dances. The schools have seen that the cultural centres could be ideal places for these forms of instruction as they could provide a focal point for the social development of students as well as helping conserve the local culture.

Local residents and teachers also recognize that the current style of school education only accelerates the loss of traditional culture, which is one of the reasons why parents are losing confidence in the school system and students are becoming tired of their studies. For decades, the Tibetan teaching materials have been translations of Chinese language books or original texts. Although courses in the Tibetan language have been set up in recent years, these course materials lack the required knowledge of traditional Tibetan culture, such as history and literature. No school-based textbooks have been developed by local people or school teachers, and there is no school-based curriculum associated with preservation of the local culture. In fact, it has only been in the last few years that the fonts for writing in the particular Rgyalrong script have been agreed by central government.

Because the local government focuses on economic development with a growth in GDP, the existing social, spiritual and cultural resources of the people are gradually being replaced by materialism. Many young Tibetan teachers are therefore no longer interested in education, and through their contacts change their professions to become civil servants. The situation is found throughout the country, but it is particularly serious in the Tibetan region. All aspects of traditional culture depend upon the social structures of a community and schools are an important part of that structure. The teachers need to be encouraged to take the initiative, together with the villagers to participate in social and cultural activities, such as celebrations, rituals and festivals.

One of the biggest problems for students who study in Tibetan is that they cannot find jobs when they graduate. They can't find a place in the modern Chinese language society, but they don't want to return to the farming or nomadic lifestyle of their parents. They are therefore stranded between these two options. No wonder many of the young men take work driving motorcycle taxis on the grasslands and look for caterpillar fungus in season. Many of the young women go to the cities or hotels to cook, sing, dance or even prostitution.

> Deng Xiaoping's reforms therefore unleashed two very different trends: on the one hand, a greater freedom to promote minority language education, with the consequence that the quality and availability of Tibetan-medium education is at present better than it has ever been; on the other hand, increasing competition in the wake of the marketization of the education system and of government employment, which is threatening to divide the Tibetan community along new class lines. (Zenz, 2008).

Schools provide the most important vehicle for the conservation of the Rgyalrong way of life, but also one of the greatest threats. It is hoped that the cultural centres might provide a focus for constructive conservation in the midst of a rapidly changing society.

16 Conservation and Change

I was once speaking to a group of Tibetan school teachers on the topic of Culture: Conservation and Change. After the talk the young men politely pressed me with the question of whether there can be a Tibetan culture without Tibetan Buddhism. This is an extremely relevant question because the Chinese authorities would prefer to promote a distinction between a modern secular and socialist Tibetan identity and that of a Tibetan identity based on Buddhism and the role of the monasteries. This policy is significant not only in making a divide between the Dalai Lama and the Tibetan people, but also it supports the CCP view of religion as a detrimental social force.

Tibetan refugees especially have voiced strong criticisms of the Chinese government accusing the authorities of wantonly destroying Tibetan culture. Chinese government media have countered these accusations by publishing extensive reports on the development of Tibetan culture under Communist rule. No one can doubt that Beijing has invested a lot of money in the Tibetan region, but it has had little influence upon the opinion of most Tibetans. In reality there is no simple black-and-white answer to the question, but a complex set of interactions which will be discussed in this final chapter.

The Civilizing Project

Stevan Harrell's (1994) framework of three successive "civilizing projects" mentioned in chapter 1 is helpful in trying to understand the enduring Chinese urge to civilize the minority peoples. These three projects are the Confucian, the Christian and the Communist (secular). As we saw, Harrell defines a civilizing project as an interaction between people in which one group (the civilizing centre) interacts with the other groups (the peripheral peoples) in an unequal relationship. This inequality provides the ideological basis for the centre's claim to a superior degree of civilization over that of the peripheral peoples. As a result, the civilizing process aims to bring those designated as "uncivilized" closer to the universal "civilization" and to bring about the associated social practices embedded in such "civilization". To understand the entire process one has to look at the culture, ethics and religion of both the civilizers and the civilizees.

The Communist civilization process, with its emphasis on revolution was strong in terms of political change, which commenced when the Chinese communist forces entered the Tibetan region in 1951. In Chinese history textbooks this is presented as the liberation of serfs from the domination and exploitation of the religious leaders and the bringing back of the region to the Motherland. Especially to the Tibetans of the diaspora, this is seen as a brutal invasion of an independent nation and the suppression of their unique way of life. Chinese Communism has certainly brought rapid social change to Tibet and in so doing has drawn a separation between their past and their present.

The most obvious expression of this change is the impact of modernity upon the people even though it is has "Chinese characteristics". The land now belongs to the nation (China) and more specifically the Chinese Communist Party (CCP). The logic continues that the land, with all its resources therefore should be used for the benefit of the nation as a whole. As it is the majority of the people living in the major cities of the East coast who are experiencing the greatest economic growth, this means the resources from the land are dictated by the needs of the great cities.

There is no doubt that massive investment has been made by the Chinese into the region. The Qinghai-Tibetan railway is unquestionably one of the greatest feats of transport engineering since the first train line from Liverpool to Manchester in 1829. The government has been aware of the need for the conservation of the wild-life on this high-altitude plateau. This project has essentially left the people of Rgyalrong untouched although proposals are still being discussed for the construction of a new high-speed line from Chengdu through the Dadu river valley to Lhasa. What however has caused the greatest impact on the ordinary people of the region have been the many hydroelectric schemes built along the Dadu River as mentioned in chapter 3.

These hydroelectric schemes have not only polluted the water so that fish no longer live in the rivers, but have brought with them massive disruption to land usage. Fields that have for generations been cultivated by the same families have now been flooded to harness the power of the water to generate electricity for far-away cities and industries. New roads have been blasted through the mountains in order to provide the needed transport links for the growing infra-structure.

Technological changes need not always be on such a massive scale to make a significant impact on the local people. For the majority of people, changes come in small ways, but the impact can have repercussions throughout the whole of their society (Foster, 1973). People quickly see the practical advantages of a cheap plastic bowl or bucket over that of the traditional vessels; cheaper clothes mass produced in the cities; new tools and vehicles to make the work easier. Perhaps the greatest change that the people of Rgyalrong have willingly adopted has been the arrival of electricity. This has not only brought light to the dark nights, but it has brought radios and televisions as a channel of information and entertainment. Electricity has also brought the cell phone as a primary means of communication to family members scattered throughout the cities of China and the mountain villages of the hinterland. Now even the monks carry a cell phone.

As was discussed in chapter 15 education has been a key element in the communist civilization process. New China needs more than farmers; it needs urban workers to continue to manufacture the products for the world market. Cheap labour coming from the countryside has been the driving force of the Chinese "economic miracle" since Reform and Opening Up in the late 1970s. Today this requires more than the physical strength of the farm workers - it needs a more educated workforce and this requires the schooling of the younger generation. The results have been many.

First, the schooling has been a secularizing force with an atheistic scientific philosophy. Mathematics, science and ethics have excluded any religious or superstitious foundation. This has not converted the young generation from a Buddhist to a secular worldview, but has resulted in a dualism of thinking that will be discussed later. Secondly, the young people have been physically separated from their families as they have had to live in the towns and cities to benefit from the 9-years of free schooling that is now provided. Thirdly, schools have physically weakened the younger generation who can no longer work in the fields as did their parents. Their hands are soft, their backs are weak and they no longer wish to work the long hours of their parents.

Whilst the engineering projects have come to the people without their approval, migration to the cities has come from their own choice to benefit from the new opportunities. Although change can often come uninvited, in many cases it is accepted and even embraced as a positive event. Many of the young people have found work in the cities and are earning money to send back to their families. However, the cost has been high and perhaps beyond that initially realized. In order to live and work in the cities the young people have had to adapt to much of modern Chinese life-style and language. The villages have gradually emptied leaving only older people and younger children. Eventually the old people will die, the children will join their parents in the cities, and the village will be no more. Prof Li Huadong reported that more than 900,000 villages in China were abandoned or destroyed in the first decade of this century. He says, "In our old rural society we had moral standards, ancestral halls and family discipline based on close-knit relationships. All this has been wiped out. The DNA of our culture is in the villages. If our villages are destroyed, Chinese people will cease to be Chinese people." (Jim Russell, 2013). This is equally true of the mountain villages of the Dadu River valley.

A past to be gained

Why do people want to preserve the past? Lowenthal argues that the past is integral to our sense of identity and is a driving force with many minority peoples in the face of global change (Lowenthal, 1994). However, one must not assume that it is possible to save the "real" past in an unchanged form. We cannot avoid remaking our heritage, for every act of recognition alters what survives. We can use the past fruitfully only when we realize that to inherit it is also to transform it. What our predecessors have left us deserves respect, but a demand to simply preserve becomes an impossible burden. The past is best used by being domesticated and by our acceptance of this fact and rejoicing in so doing. The past is not simply back there, in a separate and foreign country; it is assimilated in ourselves, and resurrected into an ever-changing present.

As was mentioned in chapter 6 in the discussion of arts and crafts, the UNESCO "Convention for the Safeguarding of the Intangible Cultural Heritage" (2003) identified five broad domains with regards to Intangible Heritage: 1) Oral traditions and expressions: language being the vehicle. 2) Performing arts. 3) Social practices, rituals and festive events. 4) Knowledge and practices concerning nature and the universe. 5) Traditional craftsmanship. It was along these lines that the research team at the Institute of Education, Sichuan Normal University sought to conserve various elements of intangible heritage among the Rgyalrongwa. The question that continued to emerge during these projects was the question of authenticity.

As was described in chapter 6, in an attempt to preserve traditional craftsmanship an old man who had the knowledge of making black pottery was encouraged to take four younger men as his apprentices. Although the old man knew the process of manufacture this did not mean that he was skilled to produce something that would be appreciated by the present generation as either being of practical value or a work of art. Unless the item has a quality that can be appreciated by later generations as meaningful and significant it has little value. This means the artefact must have an inherent quality that can be appreciated by others beyond the immediate community in time and space. This requires the apprentices to understand not only the process of manufacture, but have the "spirit" of the artistic creation. Otherwise, what is produced is merely a commodity that passing tourists might like to buy as a souvenir of their visit.

Tourism is promoted among most minority peoples as a means for economic development. Some have had greater commercial success than others at this depending on whether they have a unique social, technological or geographical advantage. Despite all the millions of tourists who travel the globe every year there are only a limited number of souvenirs a tourist will buy.

Festivals

The issue of authenticity also emerged with regards to the festivals—another element listed by UNESCO as intangible heritage. The New Year festival discussed in chapter 10 was revived by drawing on the memories of four old men who had experienced the festival more than 30 years previously. The Cultural Revolution with its emphasis on the destruction of the "Four Olds"—Old Customs, Old Culture, Old Habits, and Old Ideas caused a rejection of traditional culture that had a massive impact on China from 1965 to 1968 (Clark, 2008). What remained for the old men were their individual memories that were distorted through the suffering and trauma they had known in their past.

Although the festival was constructed from individual memories, one could not help but feel that through the very interaction between the four men new perspectives were being created and accepted as reality. Practically many of the key elements of the festival could not be reproduced. For example, there is no longer a *tusi* (king) to direct events and receive homage. The meaning of much of the symbolism was lost because the keeper of the tradition had died without passing on to others the secret knowledge. The festival that was eventually held must be acknowledged to be something of an invention—a new construct. New elements were added either by innovation or, as in some cases by accident. Nevertheless, the experience of the festival by young and old alike helped to form these individual memories into what could be considered the "collective memory" of the present community. This was later reinforced by the repetition of the festival during the following years, and through video recording the event. It should be emphasised that although the people had different motives for taking part in the festival it was definitely not something staged for outsiders. What was important for the people was the fact that it was their *own* festival and this produced a sense of pride in their distinctive identity and history. As stated earlier this is perhaps the most important aspect in the process of preservation.

Another festival that the team examined was that of marriage, one of the important rites of passage for any community. Rites of passage mark significant stages for an individual in a community as have been discussed by many writers since van Gennep (van Gennep, 1977). Generally, such rituals are less likely to change than other traits of culture because they are liminal rituals that are accepted by people as something "we just do". The civilizing projects of Christianity and Communism both sought to introduce a legal ceremony as an aspect of the marriage, but today in modern China this remains a distinct activity. The government is concerned about the legal signing of the contract of marriage and it allows freedom for people to adopt other activities, which most commonly involves a banquet for friends and family at a later date.

Thus, Rgyalrong couples first go to the government office to get the formal documentation of their marriage before having a celebratory meal with their family and friends some days or weeks later. As described in chapter 7 one project sought to encourage the local people to follow a more traditional style of ritual and celebration for a wedding. The fact that the families expected to have a celebratory meal meant that the inclusion of many of the ancient customs was something that was readily accepted. The wedding was not only photogenic, but was an event enjoyed by young and old alike. Once again, the main value was that it conserved a sense of social identity and historical continuity.

Religion

In all cultures religion is usually the trait that changes least over time. This is usually because the teaching and practices are considered to be of a higher level of wisdom than ordinary mundane skills and knowledge. There can be the occasional generation of a new religious movement that results in rapid social change, but generally the laws and practices are governed by monks, priests and scribes of the particular tradition. These keepers of the tradition guard the teachings and rituals and pass them on to the younger generation in what is presented as the authentic teaching. The importance of such knowledge means that this is the first to be written down and these texts are copied and preserved. In the Rgyalrong area it is the monasteries with their monks that are the mainstay for preserving these traditions. As illustrated at the beginning of this chapter, for many Tibetans it is Tibetan Buddhism that is the core of Tibetan culture.

Among the lamas and religious leaders, identity is rooted in different traditions of Buddhism, which at times leads to disputes and even physical conflict between the various schools of Buddhism. Most families however have little clear understanding of the doctrinal or ritual differences between the various Buddhist traditions. Their allegiance tends to be with the nearby monastery at which one of their sons may be resident. Changes however are gradually taking place and a more educated, ethical form of religion seems to be preferred. This is encouraging the spread of the *dGelugpa* ("yellow hat") tradition especially as it is more scholastic and associated with the Dali Lama.

Superstitions are usually defined as falling outside mainstream religions in lacking any clear underlying philosophy apart from the belief that in some way "like effects like". As was discussed in chapter 11 on folk religion, I tend to see "superstitions" as being on a continuum between formal religion at one axis and customs at the other. There is little doctrinal basis for superstitions - it is something that people regard as having always been practised. It is like the Englishman not walking under a ladder, or considering 13 an unlucky number. Nevertheless among the Rgyalrong these superstitions are still strongly held by the older generation, and even the young people would not neglect them. I have known university graduates eagerly buy live fish in the market with the express purpose of releasing them into the river in order to gain merit. Little thought is given for the market seller who has imperilled his own soul to capture the little fish and offer them for sale.

New forms of Identity

If the conservation of culture is primarily to retain social identity, the question remains as to what sort of social identity is preserved. Before 1950, sub-national identity was based on religious tradition or region. The first category included the Tibetan schools of Nyingma, Kargyu, Sakya, Gelugpa and Bönpa and was mainly important to the lamas. Regional identity and attachment to the homeland was more important to the laity and included areas such as Kham, Tsang and Amdo. However, since the Chinese takeover in 1959, there has been a growing consciousness, particularly among urban Tibetans, about a pan-Tibetan identity that differentiates itself from the Han Chinese.

The Han residents in the region are seen as dominating political and economic power, and having greater access to education and job opportunities within Tibet. Although Tibetans are divided over the issue of total independence or regional autonomy there has been a united resistance to Chinese domination in recent years. As Topgyal has written:

> For the Tibetan exiles too, despite the disagreements on goal and strategy, the Tibetan struggle is ultimately about their identity. Whether they are struggling for independence or autonomy through non-violence and dialogue or more aggressive tactics, the Tibetans are ultimately striving to save their identity from erasure (Topgyal, 2013).

Today, one way the young people have of retaining their distinctive identity is by adopting a dual worldview. In the classrooms with their teachers they respond with the required answers of any student in modern China. In their work in the cities they adopt Chinese practices and blend into society as far as they can. They feel as though the majority Han look down on them and they are passed over for advancement in their employment. They realize they are members of the single nation of China even though their ID card marks them out as belonging to a non-Han *minzu*. Nevertheless, when they return to their home areas or sit among Rgyalrong friends they fall into a different way of thinking. This sense of duality is the way that many Tibetans maintain their distinctive identity.

A second way is that young Tibetans living in the cities are creating a new expression of Tibetan culture based on traditional symbols and expressing their identity through popular music to create a kind of Tibetan urban subculture. The lyrics of Tibetan pop songs often wistfully describe the beauty of the Tibetan landscape or the traditional way of life. Phrases in the songs often have deeper meanings that are often missed by the casual Han listeners. One wonders how far the young urban generation can craft a culture that is Chinese on the outside, and yet retain a distinctive identity that links back to the ancient way of life of their forefathers.

One Tibetan academic has undertaken research into the question of Tibetan social identity in modern China. He interviewed many Tibetans in different levels of society. Of the young generation he concludes: "Young Tibetans feel very pessimistic about the future of Tibetan culture and see no signs that the economic, educational, or linguistic situation of ethnic Tibetans who are unwilling to abandon their cultural heritage will soon improve. They believe that the only long-term solution to their problems is an autonomous government of their own." (Nima, 2007: 128). Nima concludes:

> It seems more likely that the Chinese civilizing project will succeed: Tibetan culture will gradually be lost and the Tibetan people absorbed into the wider Han society .... But perhaps both the disappearance of Tibetan culture and violent conflict can be avoided through reform of the education system. If education is central to the problem of Tibetan identity, perhaps it could also be central to the solution: a new type of school might be developed that draws directly upon Tibetan skills and philosophy such that it becomes an integral part of the life of the people. Traditional techniques and practices need to be recorded and young people encouraged to learn them from the older artisans before they are lost. Young people, likewise, need to regain a pride in their ancestral culture while seeking creative ways to put its strengths to use in the modern world. Tourism, for example, could both provide economic benefit and assist Tibetans in preserving their heritage." (Nima, 2007: 128).

This book has sought to study the conservation of aspects of the Rgyalrong way of life in the midst of the Communist civilizing process. Some aspects have succeeded to a degree, but what is clear is that their culture will change. Tibetan culture can't be held as in some museum. Western people also need to cut through the vision of a spiritual idyllic nation on the roof of the world. Popular Hollywood films like *Seven Years in Tibet* and *Kundun* have presented the world with an image of Tibet that reinforces stereotypes of a land and people so "other" that they are seen by some as redeemers of a depraved modern world (D. Lopez, 1998).

Tibetans need to be respected as members of a unique and distinct culture, and one that is taking its place in the modern world. Neither must minority cultures be considered merely as objects to be civilized, but the people should be allowed to express their own distinctive identity among the societies of the world. This requires a continual balance between conservation and change, but above all in the twenty-first century the people of Tibet need to be respected for who they are.

Bibliography

Alexander, A. (2013). *The Traditional Lhasa House: Typology of an Endangered Species*. Habitat-International.

Antze, P. & Lambek, M. (1996). *Tense Past*. London: Routledge.

Appadurai, A. (1986). Introduction: Commodities and the Politics of Value. In A. Appadurai (Ed.), *The Social Life of Things - Commodities in Cultural Perspective* (pp. 3–63). Cambridge: Cambridge University Press.

Bansal, B. L. (1994). *Bon: Its encounter with Buddhism in Tibet*. Delhi: Eastern Book Linkers.

Batchelor, S. (1998). Letting daylight into magic: the life and times of Dorje Shugden. *Tricycle: The Buddhist Review*, 60–66.

Baumer, C. (2013). *Bon: Tibet's Ancient Religion*. Thailand: Orchid Press.

Bellezza, J. V. (2009). Flight of the Khyung (2009)| Tibet Archaeology. *Tibetan Archaeology*. Retrieved from http://www.tibetarchaeology. com/august-2009/

Bellezza, J. V. (2010). gShen-rab Myi-bo, His life and times according to Tibet's earliest literary sources. *Revue d'Etudes Tibétaines*, *19*, 31–118.

Berga, L. (2006). *Dams and Reservoirs, Societies and Environment in the 21ˢᵗ Century*. Barcelona.

Berliner, N. (2012). *Yin Yu Tang: The Architecture and Daily Life of a Chinese House: A Traditional Chinese House*. Turtle Publishing.

Bicker, A. Pottier, J, Sillitoe, P. (2002). *Participating in Development: Approaches to Indigenous Knowledge*. London: Routledge.

Braudel, F. (1993). *A History of Civilizations*. New York: Penguin.

Brauen, M. (1982). Death Customs in Ladakh. *Kailash-Journal of Himalayan Studies*, 319–332.

Brian J. (1999). Review: Tsundu: Becoming a Lama by Raju Mani Gurung. *American Anthropological Society, 101*(3), 635–9.

Burnett, D. (2005). *World of the Spirits*. Oxford: Monarch.

Carstein, J. H.-J. S. (Ed.). (1995). *About the House: Levi-Strauss and Beyond*. Cambridge: Cambridge University Press.

Catriona Bass. (1998). *Education in Tibet: Policy and Practice since 1950*. London: Zed Books.

Catriona Bass. (2005). Learning to love the motherland: educating Tibetans in China. *Journal of Moral Education, 34*(4), 433–449.

Chang, Jung. Halliday, J. (2005). *Mao: The Unknown Story*. London: Jonathan Cape.

Chen, K. Y. (1997, July 11). Speech on Literature and Art. *Tibet Daily*. Lhasa.

Cheng Yu Wai, I. (2003). *A Socio-cultural study of Kaiping watchtowers*. University of Hong Kong.

Chogyal Namkai Norbu & D. Rossi. (2013). *History of Zhang Zheng and Tibet: Volume One: the Early Period*. North Atlantic Books.

Clark, P. (2008). *The Chinese Cultural Revolution: A History*. Cambridge University Press.

Cohen, E. (1988). Authenticity and Commoditization in Tourism. *Annals of Tourism Research, 15*, 371–386.

Coleman, W. (2002). The Uprising at Batang: Khams and its significance in Chinese and Tibetan history. In L. Epstein (Ed.), *Khampa Histories* (pp. 31–55). Leiden: Brill.

Connerton, P. (1989). *How Societies Remember*. Cambridge: Cambridge University Press.

Convention Between Great Britain, China, and Tibet, Simla (1914). (1914). *Tibet Justice Center - Legal Materials on Tibet - Treaties and Conventions Relating to Tibet*. Retrieved March 14, 2014, from http://www.tibetjustice.org/materials/treaties/treaties16.html

Coser, L. A. (1992). *Maurice Halbwachs: On Collective Memory*. Chicago: University of Chicago Press.

Dai Min. (2010). *Research on Tourism Development of Danba Jiaju Tibetan Village through Tourism Anthropology.* Sichuan Normal University.

Darragon, F. (2006). *Secret Towers of the Himalayas* (pp. 1–156). Unicorn Foundation.

Darragon, F. (2008). *About Carbon Dating techniques in general and my use of that technique to date 68 ancient towers found in Sichuan and Tibet* (pp. 12–15).

Darragon, F. (2008). The Secret Towers of the Himalayas. China.

Darragon, F. (2009). The Star-shaped Towers of the Tribal Corridor of Southwest China. *Journal of Cambridge Studies, 4*(2), 67–83.

Dawa Norbu. (1979). The 1959 Tibetan Rebellion : An Interpretation. *The China Quarterly, 77*(77), 74–93.

Deqi Shan. (2011). *Chinese Vernacular Dwellings (Introductions to Chinese Culture).* Cambridge University Press.

Dreyfus, G. B. J. (2003). *The Sound of Two Hands Clapping: The Education of a Tibetan Buddhist Monk.* University of California Press.

Eliade, M. (1971). *The Myth of the Eternal Return.* London: Taylor & Francis.

Eliade, M. (1991). Symbolism of the Centre. In *Images and Symbols.* Princeton: Princeton University Press.

Elliott, C. 尼西黑陶: A Study of Tibetan Black Pottery., Independent Study Project (ISP) Collection (2011). Retrieved from http://digitalcollections.sit.edu/isp_collection/1075

Ewing, S. (2003). Traditions of Appearance : Adaptation and Change in Eastern Tibetan Dwellings. *International Association for the Study of Traditional Environments (IASTE), 15*(1), 73–84.

Flower, J. W. M. (2004). A Road is Made: Roads, Temples and Historical Memory in Ya'an County, Sichuan. *The Journal of Asian Studies, 63*(3), 649–685.

Foster, G. M. (1973). *Traditional Societies and Technological Change* (2nd edition). London: Harper Row.

French, P. (1994). *Younghusband: The Last Great Imperial Adventurer.* London: Harper Collins.

Given, B. J. (1997). Review of "Tsundu: Becoming a Lama." *American Anthropologist, 101*(3), 636–7.

Goldstein, M. C. (1997). *The Snow Lion and the Dragon: China, Tibet, and the Dalai Lama.* University of California Press.

Graham, D. C. (1958). *The Customs and Religion of the Ch'iang.* Washington: Smithsonian Institute.

Gyu 'brung & Stuard, C. K. (2012). Rgyal Rong Tibetan Life, Language, and in Rgyas Bzang Village. *Asian Highlands Perspectivess, 15,* 140–150.

Harrell, S. (1995). Introduction: Civilizing projects and the reaction to them. In S. Harrell (Ed.), *Cultural Encounters on China's Ethnic Frontier* (pp. 3–36). Seattle and London: University of Washington Press.

Harrell, S. (1995). *Cultural Encounters on China's Ethnic Frontiers.* University of Washington Press.

Hattaway, P. (1990). *Operation China* (Third edit.). Piquant.

Hendry, J. (2005). *Reclaiming Culture: Indigenous People and Self-Representation.* London: Palgrave.

Huarui & Dongshi. (2001, May). Worship the gods by smoke. *Tibet.*

Jianping, Q., Hongling, T., & Xinpo, L. (2006). Analysis of Danba landslide. *Wuhan University Journal of Natural Sciences.* doi:10.1007/BF02830181

Jim Russell. (2013). Rural China Is Dying - Pacific Standard: The Science of Society. *Pacific Standard.* Retrieved March 07, 2014, from http://www.psmag.com/navigation/business-economics/burgh-disapora/rural-china-dying-70578/

Jisheng, X. (2001). The Mythology of Tibetan Mountain Gods : An Overview. *Oral Tradition, 2,* 343–363.

Johnson, Bonnie, N. C. (2002). Exclusionary Policies and Practices in Chinese Minority Education: The Case of Tibetan Education. *Current Issues in Comparative Education, 2*(2), 142–153.

Jun Jing. (1996). *The Temple of Memories: History, Power and Morality in a Chinese Village*. Stanford University Press.

Kapstein, M. (2006). *The Tibetans*. Oxford: Blackwell.

Karmay, S. G. (1972). *The treasury of good sayings: a Tibetan history of Bon*. London, etc.: Oxford University Press.

Karmay, S. G. (1986). Origin and early development of the Tibetan religious traditions of the Great Perfection (Rdzogs Chen). [electronic resource]. University of London.

Karmay, S. G. (1996). The Cult of Mount Murdo in Gyalrong. *Kailash-Journal of Himalayan Studies, 18*(1 & 2).

Karmay, S. G. (1998). *The arrow and the spindle : studies in history, myths, rituals and beliefs in Tibet* (1ˢᵗ ed.). Kathmandu: Mandala Book Point.

Karmay, S. G. (2005). *Feast of the morning light : the eighteenth century wood-engravings of Shenrab's life-stories and the Bon Canon from Gyalrong*. Osaka: National Museum of Ethnology.

Karmay, S. G. (2005). The Great Fifth. *IIAS Newsletter, 39*, 12–15.

Karmay, S. G., & Nagano, Y. (2000). *New horizons in Bon studies*. Osaka: National Museum of Ethnology.

Knapp, R. G. (2005). *Chinese Houses: The Architectural Heritage of a Nation*. Turtle Publishing.

Kolas, A. (2005). *Ethnic Tourism in Shangrila: Representations of Place and Tibetan Identity*. Oslo: University of Oslo.

Kvaerne, P. (1974). The canon of the Tibetan Bonpos. *Indo-Iranian Journal, 16*(2), 96–144.

Kværne, P. (1995). *The Bon religion of Tibet: the iconography of a living tradition*. London: Brill.

Lakhu, Libu, Stuart, C.K. & Roche, G. (2009). Calling back the lost Tibetan soul. *Asian Highlands Perspectives, 1*, 65–115.

Lane, F. (1994). The Warrior Tribes of Kham. *Asiaweek*, 30–38.

Levi-Strauss, C. (1982). *The Way of the Mask*. Seattle: University of Washington Press.

Li, M. (1990). Moral education in the People's Republic of China. *Journal of Moral Education, 19*(3), 159–170.

Liu Yaling. (2009). Pilgrimage and Circumambulation - Examination of Tibetan Pilgrimage in Danba. *South-Central Nationalities University Journal, 29*(2), 55–59.

Lopez, D. (1998). *Prisoners of Shangri-La: Tibetan Buddhism and the West.* Chicago: University of Chicago Press.

Lopez, D. S. (1996). " Lamaism " and the Disappearance of Tibet. *Comparative Studies in Society and History, 38*(1), 3–25.

Lowenthal, D. (1994). *The Past is a Foreign Country.* Cambridge: Cambridge University Press.

Ma, R. (2010). The Soviet Model's Influence and the Current Debate on Ethnic Relations. *Global Asia,* 50–55.

MacCannell, D. (1973). Staged Authenticity: Arrangements of Social Space in Tourist Settings. *American Journal of Sociology, 79*(3), 589–603.

Madsen, R. (2010). The upsurge of religion in China. *Journal of Democracy, 21*(4), 58–72.

Markowitz, S. J. (1994). The Distinction Between Art and Craft. *Journal of Aesthetic Education, 28*(1), 55–70.

Martin, D. (1990). Bonpo Canons and Jesuit Cannons: On Sectarian Factors involved in the Chien-lung Emperor's Second Goldstream Expedition of 1771-1776. *The Tibet Journal, 15*(2), 3–28.

Martin, D. (2013). On the Cultural Ecology of Sky Burial on the Himalayan Plateau. *East and West, 46*(3), 353–370.

Martin, D. A. N. (1996). Unearthing Bon Treasures: A Study of Tibetan Sources. *Journal of American Oriental Society, 116*(4), 619–644.

Michaud, J. (2010). Editorial - Zomia and Beyond. *Journal of Global History, 5,* 187–214.

Miller, B. D. (1961). The Web of Tibetan Monasteries. *The Journal of Asian Studies, 20*(2), 197–203.

Mills, M. A. (2000). Vajra Brother, Vajra Sister: Renunciation, Individualism and the Household in Tibetan Buddhist Monasticism. *Journal of the Royal Anthropological Insitute, 6*(1), 17–34.

Nakh architecture. (2013). *Wikipedia.* Retrieved from http://en.wikipedia.org/wiki/Nakh_Architecture

Nima, B. (2007). Tibetan Identity in Today's China. In J. L. Peacock, P. Horton, & P. Inman (Eds.), *Identity Matters: Ethnic and Sectarian Conflict* (Vol. 37, pp. 120–129). Berghahn Books.

Nima Baden. (1997). The Way out for Tibetan Education. *Chinese Education & Society, 30*(4), 7–21.

Oakes, T. (1998). *Tourism and Modernity in China*. London: Routledge.

Obeyesekere, G. (1963). The Great Tradition and the Little in Perspective of Sinhalese Buddhism. *Journal of Asian Studies, 22,* 139–153.

Pallis, M. (1967). Introduction to Tibetan Art. *Studies in Comparative Religion, 1*(1), 17–26.

Peissel, M. (1972). *Cavaliers of Kham: The Secret War in Tibet*. London: Heinemann.

Pelliot, Paul & Chavannes, E. (1911). Un traité manichéen retrouvé en Chine. *Journal Asiatique,* 499–617.

Prins, M. (2006). The Rgyalrong New Year: A case history of changing identity. In *Tibetan Borderlands* (pp. 1–27). Leiden: Brill.

Prins, M. (2007). Speechmaking: Contextualized Teaching in the Rgyalrong Culture, 1–39.

Qing Imperial Polearms. (n.d.). Retrieved March 27, 2014, from http://thomaschen.freewebspace.com/photo4.html

Raji Mani Gurung. (1997). *Tsundu: Becoming a Lama - Film*.

Ramble, C. (1982). Status and Death: Mortuary Rites and attitudes to the body in a Tibetan village. *Kailash-Journal of Himalayan Studies*.

Rao, J. (2005, December). Moon to hide beautiful star cluster. *Nightsky Friday*.

Redfield, R. (1956). *Peasant Society and Culture*. Chicago: University of Chicago Press.

Rinchen rdo rje & Kevin, C. (2009). Seating, Money and Food at an Amdo Village Funeral. *Asian Highland Perspectives, 1,* 237–294.

Samuel, G. (1993). *Civilized Shamans: Buddhism in Tibetan Society* (p. 718). Washington & London: Smithsonian Institute Press.

Scharf, A, et. al. (2013). AMS Dating of Wooden Cores From Historic Buildings. *Radiocarbon, 55*(2), 1358–1365.

Schrempf, M., & Hayes, J. P. (2009). From Temple to Commodity? Tourism in Songpan and the Bon Monasteries of Amdo Shar khog. *East and West, 59*(1), 285–312.

Scott, J. W. (2009). *The Art of not being Governed: An Anarchist history of Upland Southeast Asia.* New Haven, CT.: Yale University Press.

Semple, W. (2005). Traditional Architecture in Tibet: Linking Issues of Environmental and Cultural Sustainability. *Moutain Research and Development, 25*(1), 15–19.

Sillitoe, P. (2007). Anthropologists only need apply: challenges of applied anthropology. *JRAI, 13.*

Singh, R. K. (2009). Indigenous knowledge of yak breeding and management by Brokpa community in eastern Himalaya, Arunachal Pradesh. *Indian Journal of Traditional Knowledge, 8*(October), 495–501.

Skorupski, T. (1982). The Cremation Ceremony According to the Byang-gter Tradition. *Kailash, 9*(4), 361–376.

Smith, M. R. D. (2003). *The Ethics of Tourism.* London: Routledge.

Snellgrove, D. & Richardson, H. (1986). *A Cultural History of Tibet.* Boston & London: Shambala.

Snow, E. (1978). *Red Star over China.* London: Bantam Books.

Stalin, J. (1913). The National Question and Social-Democracy. *Prosveshcheniye, 3,* 300–381.

Stein, R. A. (1972). *Tibetan Civilization.* London: Faber.

Studley, J. (2007). *Hearing a Different Drummer: A new paradigm for the "keeper of the forest."* London: IIED.

Tang, W., & He, G. (2010). *Separate but Loyal : Ethnicity and Nationalism in China.* Honolulu: East-West Centre.

Terwiel, B. J. (1994). *Monks and Magic: An Analysis of Religious Ceremonies in Central Thailand.* Bangkok: White Lotus.

Thomas, A. (1999). Overview of the Gongga Shan Range, Sichuan Province, China. *Mountain Research and Development, 19*(1), 17–30.

Thupten Phentsok & Tsewang Lhamo. (2009). *Study in Elements of Tibetan Medicine.* Beijing: China Tibetology Publishing House.

Topgyal, T. (2013, September 1). *Identity Insecurity and the Tibetan Resistance Against China. Pacific Affairs.* London School of Economics. Retrieved from http://openurl.ingenta.com/content/ xref?genre=article&issn=0030-851X&volume=86&issue=3&sp age=515

Tshe Mdo. (2009). Lazi (lab rtse) Construction in Karmatang. *Asian Highlands Perspectives, 1,* 349–366.

Tsomo, K. L. (2001). Death, Identity, and Enlightenment. *International Journal of Transpersonal Studies, 20,* 151–173.

Tucci, G. (1980). *The Religions of Tibet.* London: Routledge & Kegan Paul.

UNESCO. (2013). Diablo Buildings and villages for Tibetan and Qiang Ethnic Groups. *UNESCO.* Retrieved from http://whc.unesco.org/ fr/listesindicatives/5815/

Upton, J. (1999). The Development of Modern School-Based Tibetan Language Education in the PRC. In G.A. Postiglione (Ed.), *China's national minority education: Culture, schooling and development.* New York: Falmer Press.

Urry, J. (1990). *The Tourist Gaze: Leisure and Travel in Contemporary Societies* (p. 176). London: SAGE Publications.

Van Driem, G. (2001). *Languages of the Himalayas: an ethnolinguistic handbook of the Greater Himalayan Region containing an introduction to the symbiotic theory of language.* Leiden: Brill.

Van Gennep, A. (1977). *The Rites of Passage.* University of Chicago Press.

Vergata, T. (2008). *Sichuan Towers : Sustainable Conservation and Enhancement* (pp. 1–13). Rome.

Vinding, M. (1982). The Thakalis as Buddhists: A closer look at their death ceremonies. *Kailash, 4*(9), 291–318.

Waley-Cohen, J. (1998). Religion, War, and Empire-Building China Eighteenth-Century. *The International History Review, 20*(2), 336–352.

Wang, M.-K. (2002, January 1). Searching for Qiang Culture in the First Half of the Twentieth Century. *Inner Asia.* Brill.

Wang, X. (2011). *China's Last Imperial Frontier: Late Qing Expansion in Sichuan's Tibetan Borderlands*. Lexington Books.

Waterson, R. (2012). *The Living House: An Anthropology of Architecture in South-East Asia*. London: Turtle Publishing.

Wellens, K. (2010). *Religious revival in the Tibetan borderlands the Premi of southwest China* (p. 278). Seattle: University of Washington Press,.

Wertsch, J. C. (2002). *Voices of Collective Remembering*. Cambridge: Cambridge University Press.

When the Dust Settles. (n.d.). China.

Winkler, D. (2008). The Mushrooming Fungi Market in Tibet Exemplified by Cordyceps sinensis and Tricholoma matsutake. *Journal of the International Assocation of Tibetan Studies*, (4), 1–46.

Xie Jisheng, & Jisheng, X. (2001). The Mythology of Tibetan Mountain Gods. *Oral Tradition*, *16*(2), 343–363.

Yang Jiaming. (2004). *Country of a Thousand Towers: Danba*. CSC Books - in Chinese.

Yang, S., Zhang, H., Mao, H., Yan, D., Lu, S., Lian, L., … Gou, X. (2011). The local origin of the Tibetan pig and additional insights into the origin of Asian pigs. *PloS One*, *6*(12), e28215. Retrieved from http://www.pubmedcentral.nih.gov/articlerender. fcgi?artid=3233571&tool=pmcentrez&rendertype=abstract

Yartsa Gunbu Cordyceps | Mushroaming - Daniel Winkler's Webpages Dedicated to Mushrooms and Nature Tours. (n.d.). Retrieved from http://mushroaming.com/Yartsa_Gunbu_Cordyceps

Zenz, A. (2008). Tibetan Minority Education in Qinghai.

中国非物质文化遗产网. (2006). Retrieved from http://www.chinaich. com.cn/

www.ingramcontent.com/pod-product-compliance
Lightning Source LLC
Chambersburg PA
CBHW030431290526
45786CB00001B/239